MW01486999

*This is your*
*PASSBOOK for...*

# Principal Account Clerk

*Test Preparation Study Guide*
*Questions & Answers*

**NATIONAL LEARNING CORPORATION** ®

# COPYRIGHT NOTICE

Copyright © 2024 by
## National Learning Corporation

212 Michael Drive, Syosset, NY 11791
(516) 921-8888 • www.passbooks.com
E-mail: info@passbooks.com

PUBLISHED IN THE UNITED STATES OF AMERICA

# PASSBOOK® SERIES

THE *PASSBOOK® SERIES* has been created to prepare applicants and candidates for the ultimate academic battlefield – the examination room.

At some time in our lives, each and every one of us may be required to take an examination – for validation, matriculation, admission, qualification, registration, certification, or licensure.

Based on the assumption that every applicant or candidate has met the basic formal educational standards, has taken the required number of courses, and read the necessary texts, the *PASSBOOK® SERIES* furnishes the one special preparation which may assure passing with confidence, instead of failing with insecurity. Examination questions – together with answers – are furnished as the basic vehicle for study so that the mysteries of the examination and its compounding difficulties may be eliminated or diminished by a sure method.

This book is meant to help you pass your examination provided that you qualify and are serious in your objective.

The entire field is reviewed through the huge store of content information which is succinctly presented through a provocative and challenging approach – the question-and-answer method.

A climate of success is established by furnishing the correct answers at the end of each test.

You soon learn to recognize types of questions, forms of questions, and patterns of questioning. You may even begin to anticipate expected outcomes.

You perceive that many questions are repeated or adapted so that you can gain acute insights, which may enable you to score many sure points.

You learn how to confront new questions, or types of questions, and to attack them confidently and work out the correct answers.

You note objectives and emphases, and recognize pitfalls and dangers, so that you may make positive educational adjustments.

Moreover, you are kept fully informed in relation to new concepts, methods, practices, and directions in the field.

You discover that you are actually taking the examination all the time: you are preparing for the examination by "taking" an examination, not by reading extraneous and/or supererogatory textbooks.

In short, this PASSBOOK®, used directedly, should be an important factor in helping you to pass your test.

# PRINCIPAL ACCOUNT CLERK

DUTIES
   Performs highly difficult and responsible clerical work involving the application of bookkeeping principles and practices in the supervision and or maintenance of financial records and accounts; performs related duties as required.

SUBJECT OF EXAMINATION
   The written test designed to evaluate knowledge, skills and /or abilities in the following areas:
   1. Fundamentals of account keeping and bookkeeping;
   2. Supervision;
   3. Understanding and interpreting tabular material; and
   4. Understanding and interpreting written material.

# HOW TO TAKE A TEST

## I. YOU MUST PASS AN EXAMINATION

### A. WHAT EVERY CANDIDATE SHOULD KNOW

Examination applicants often ask us for help in preparing for the written test. What can I study in advance? What kinds of questions will be asked? How will the test be given? How will the papers be graded?

As an applicant for a civil service examination, you may be wondering about some of these things. Our purpose here is to suggest effective methods of advance study and to describe civil service examinations.

Your chances for success on this examination can be increased if you know how to prepare. Those "pre-examination jitters" can be reduced if you know what to expect. You can even experience an adventure in good citizenship if you know why civil service exams are given.

### B. WHY ARE CIVIL SERVICE EXAMINATIONS GIVEN?

Civil service examinations are important to you in two ways. As a citizen, you want public jobs filled by employees who know how to do their work. As a job seeker, you want a fair chance to compete for that job on an equal footing with other candidates. The best-known means of accomplishing this two-fold goal is the competitive examination.

Exams are widely publicized throughout the nation. They may be administered for jobs in federal, state, city, municipal, town or village governments or agencies.

Any citizen may apply, with some limitations, such as the age or residence of applicants. Your experience and education may be reviewed to see whether you meet the requirements for the particular examination. When these requirements exist, they are reasonable and applied consistently to all applicants. Thus, a competitive examination may cause you some uneasiness now, but it is your privilege and safeguard.

### C. HOW ARE CIVIL SERVICE EXAMS DEVELOPED?

Examinations are carefully written by trained technicians who are specialists in the field known as "psychological measurement," in consultation with recognized authorities in the field of work that the test will cover. These experts recommend the subject matter areas or skills to be tested; only those knowledges or skills important to your success on the job are included. The most reliable books and source materials available are used as references. Together, the experts and technicians judge the difficulty level of the questions.

Test technicians know how to phrase questions so that the problem is clearly stated. Their ethics do not permit "trick" or "catch" questions. Questions may have been tried out on sample groups, or subjected to statistical analysis, to determine their usefulness.

Written tests are often used in combination with performance tests, ratings of training and experience, and oral interviews. All of these measures combine to form the best-known means of finding the right person for the right job.

## II. HOW TO PASS THE WRITTEN TEST

### A. NATURE OF THE EXAMINATION

To prepare intelligently for civil service examinations, you should know how they differ from school examinations you have taken. In school you were assigned certain definite pages to read or subjects to cover. The examination questions were quite detailed and usually emphasized memory. Civil service exams, on the other hand, try to discover your present ability to perform the duties of a position, plus your potentiality to learn these duties. In other words, a civil service exam attempts to predict how successful you will be. Questions cover such a broad area that they cannot be as minute and detailed as school exam questions.

In the public service similar kinds of work, or positions, are grouped together in one "class." This process is known as *position-classification*. All the positions in a class are paid according to the salary range for that class. One class title covers all of these positions, and they are all tested by the same examination.

### B. FOUR BASIC STEPS

#### 1) Study the announcement

How, then, can you know what subjects to study? Our best answer is: "Learn as much as possible about the class of positions for which you've applied." The exam will test the knowledge, skills and abilities needed to do the work.

Your most valuable source of information about the position you want is the official exam announcement. This announcement lists the training and experience qualifications. Check these standards and apply only if you come reasonably close to meeting them.

The brief description of the position in the examination announcement offers some clues to the subjects which will be tested. Think about the job itself. Review the duties in your mind. Can you perform them, or are there some in which you are rusty? Fill in the blank spots in your preparation.

Many jurisdictions preview the written test in the exam announcement by including a section called "Knowledge and Abilities Required," "Scope of the Examination," or some similar heading. Here you will find out specifically what fields will be tested.

#### 2) Review your own background

Once you learn in general what the position is all about, and what you need to know to do the work, ask yourself which subjects you already know fairly well and which need improvement. You may wonder whether to concentrate on improving your strong areas or on building some background in your fields of weakness. When the announcement has specified "some knowledge" or "considerable knowledge," or has used adjectives like "beginning principles of..." or "advanced ... methods," you can get a clue as to the number and difficulty of questions to be asked in any given field. More questions, and hence broader coverage, would be included for those subjects which are more important in the work. Now weigh your strengths and weaknesses against the job requirements and prepare accordingly.

#### 3) Determine the level of the position

Another way to tell how intensively you should prepare is to understand the level of the job for which you are applying. Is it the entering level? In other words, is this the position in which beginners in a field of work are hired? Or is it an intermediate or advanced level? Sometimes this is indicated by such words as "Junior" or "Senior" in the class title. Other jurisdictions use Roman numerals to designate the level – Clerk I, Clerk II, for example. The word "Supervisor" sometimes appears in the title. If the level is not indicated by the title, check the description of duties. Will you be working under very close supervision, or will you have responsibility for independent decisions in this work?

## 4) Choose appropriate study materials

Now that you know the subjects to be examined and the relative amount of each subject to be covered, you can choose suitable study materials. For beginning level jobs, or even advanced ones, if you have a pronounced weakness in some aspect of your training, read a modern, standard textbook in that field. Be sure it is up to date and has general coverage. Such books are normally available at your library, and the librarian will be glad to help you locate one. For entry-level positions, questions of appropriate difficulty are chosen – neither highly advanced questions, nor those too simple. Such questions require careful thought but not advanced training.

If the position for which you are applying is technical or advanced, you will read more advanced, specialized material. If you are already familiar with the basic principles of your field, elementary textbooks would waste your time. Concentrate on advanced textbooks and technical periodicals. Think through the concepts and review difficult problems in your field.

These are all general sources. You can get more ideas on your own initiative, following these leads. For example, training manuals and publications of the government agency which employs workers in your field can be useful, particularly for technical and professional positions. A letter or visit to the government department involved may result in more specific study suggestions, and certainly will provide you with a more definite idea of the exact nature of the position you are seeking.

## III. KINDS OF TESTS

Tests are used for purposes other than measuring knowledge and ability to perform specified duties. For some positions, it is equally important to test ability to make adjustments to new situations or to profit from training. In others, basic mental abilities not dependent on information are essential. Questions which test these things may not appear as pertinent to the duties of the position as those which test for knowledge and information. Yet they are often highly important parts of a fair examination. For very general questions, it is almost impossible to help you direct your study efforts. What we can do is to point out some of the more common of these general abilities needed in public service positions and describe some typical questions.

### 1) General information

Broad, general information has been found useful for predicting job success in some kinds of work. This is tested in a variety of ways, from vocabulary lists to questions about current events. Basic background in some field of work, such as sociology or economics, may be sampled in a group of questions. Often these are principles which have become familiar to most persons through exposure rather than through formal training. It is difficult to advise you how to study for these questions; being alert to the world around you is our best suggestion.

### 2) Verbal ability

An example of an ability needed in many positions is verbal or language ability. Verbal ability is, in brief, the ability to use and understand words. Vocabulary and grammar tests are typical measures of this ability. Reading comprehension or paragraph interpretation questions are common in many kinds of civil service tests. You are given a paragraph of written material and asked to find its central meaning.

### 3) Numerical ability

Number skills can be tested by the familiar arithmetic problem, by checking paired lists of numbers to see which are alike and which are different, or by interpreting charts and graphs. In the latter test, a graph may be printed in the test booklet which you are asked to use as the basis for answering questions.

### 4) Observation

A popular test for law-enforcement positions is the observation test. A picture is shown to you for several minutes, then taken away. Questions about the picture test your ability to observe both details and larger elements.

### 5) Following directions

In many positions in the public service, the employee must be able to carry out written instructions dependably and accurately. You may be given a chart with several columns, each column listing a variety of information. The questions require you to carry out directions involving the information given in the chart.

### 6) Skills and aptitudes

Performance tests effectively measure some manual skills and aptitudes. When the skill is one in which you are trained, such as typing or shorthand, you can practice. These tests are often very much like those given in business school or high school courses. For many of the other skills and aptitudes, however, no short-time preparation can be made. Skills and abilities natural to you or that you have developed throughout your lifetime are being tested.

Many of the general questions just described provide all the data needed to answer the questions and ask you to use your reasoning ability to find the answers. Your best preparation for these tests, as well as for tests of facts and ideas, is to be at your physical and mental best. You, no doubt, have your own methods of getting into an exam-taking mood and keeping "in shape." The next section lists some ideas on this subject.

## IV. KINDS OF QUESTIONS

Only rarely is the "essay" question, which you answer in narrative form, used in civil service tests. Civil service tests are usually of the short-answer type. Full instructions for answering these questions will be given to you at the examination. But in case this is your first experience with short-answer questions and separate answer sheets, here is what you need to know:

### 1) Multiple-choice Questions

Most popular of the short-answer questions is the "multiple choice" or "best answer" question. It can be used, for example, to test for factual knowledge, ability to solve problems or judgment in meeting situations found at work.

A multiple-choice question is normally one of three types—

- It can begin with an incomplete statement followed by several possible endings. You are to find the one ending which *best* completes the statement, although some of the others may not be entirely wrong.
- It can also be a complete statement in the form of a question which is answered by choosing one of the statements listed.

• It can be in the form of a problem – again you select the best answer.

Here is an example of a multiple-choice question with a discussion which should give you some clues as to the method for choosing the right answer:

When an employee has a complaint about his assignment, the action which will *best* help him overcome his difficulty is to
- A. discuss his difficulty with his coworkers
- B. take the problem to the head of the organization
- C. take the problem to the person who gave him the assignment
- D. say nothing to anyone about his complaint

In answering this question, you should study each of the choices to find which is best. Consider choice "A" – Certainly an employee may discuss his complaint with fellow employees, but no change or improvement can result, and the complaint remains unresolved. Choice "B" is a poor choice since the head of the organization probably does not know what assignment you have been given, and taking your problem to him is known as "going over the head" of the supervisor. The supervisor, or person who made the assignment, is the person who can clarify it or correct any injustice. Choice "C" is, therefore, correct. To say nothing, as in choice "D," is unwise. Supervisors have and interest in knowing the problems employees are facing, and the employee is seeking a solution to his problem.

## 2) True/False Questions

The "true/false" or "right/wrong" form of question is sometimes used. Here a complete statement is given. Your job is to decide whether the statement is right or wrong.

SAMPLE: A roaming cell-phone call to a nearby city costs less than a non-roaming call to a distant city.

This statement is wrong, or false, since roaming calls are more expensive.

This is not a complete list of all possible question forms, although most of the others are variations of these common types. You will always get complete directions for answering questions. Be sure you understand *how* to mark your answers – ask questions until you do.


## V. RECORDING YOUR ANSWERS

Computer terminals are used more and more today for many different kinds of exams.

For an examination with very few applicants, you may be told to record your answers in the test booklet itself. Separate answer sheets are much more common. If this separate answer sheet is to be scored by machine – and this is often the case – it is highly important that you mark your answers correctly in order to get credit.

An electronic scoring machine is often used in civil service offices because of the speed with which papers can be scored. Machine-scored answer sheets must be marked with a pencil, which will be given to you. This pencil has a high graphite content which responds to the electronic scoring machine. As a matter of fact, stray dots may register as answers, so do not let your pencil rest on the answer sheet while you are pondering the correct answer. Also, if your pencil lead breaks or is otherwise defective, ask for another.

Since the answer sheet will be dropped in a slot in the scoring machine, be careful not to bend the corners or get the paper crumpled.

The answer sheet normally has five vertical columns of numbers, with 30 numbers to a column. These numbers correspond to the question numbers in your test booklet. After each number, going across the page are four or five pairs of dotted lines. These short dotted lines have small letters or numbers above them. The first two pairs may also have a "T" or "F" above the letters. This indicates that the first two pairs only are to be used if the questions are of the true-false type. If the questions are multiple choice, disregard the "T" and "F" and pay attention only to the small letters or numbers.

Answer your questions in the manner of the sample that follows:

32. The largest city in the United States is
   A. Washington, D.C.
   B. New York City
   C. Chicago
   D. Detroit
   E. San Francisco

1) Choose the answer you think is best. (New York City is the largest, so "B" is correct.)
2) Find the row of dotted lines numbered the same as the question you are answering. (Find row number 32)
3) Find the pair of dotted lines corresponding to the answer. (Find the pair of lines under the mark "B.")
4) Make a solid black mark between the dotted lines.

## VI. BEFORE THE TEST

Common sense will help you find procedures to follow to get ready for an examination. Too many of us, however, overlook these sensible measures. Indeed, nervousness and fatigue have been found to be the most serious reasons why applicants fail to do their best on civil service tests. Here is a list of reminders:

- Begin your preparation early – Don't wait until the last minute to go scurrying around for books and materials or to find out what the position is all about.
- Prepare continuously – An hour a night for a week is better than an all-night cram session. This has been definitely established. What is more, a night a week for a month will return better dividends than crowding your study into a shorter period of time.
- Locate the place of the exam – You have been sent a notice telling you when and where to report for the examination. If the location is in a different town or otherwise unfamiliar to you, it would be well to inquire the best route and learn something about the building.
- Relax the night before the test – Allow your mind to rest. Do not study at all that night. Plan some mild recreation or diversion; then go to bed early and get a good night's sleep.
- Get up early enough to make a leisurely trip to the place for the test – This way unforeseen events, traffic snarls, unfamiliar buildings, etc. will not upset you.
- Dress comfortably – A written test is not a fashion show. You will be known by number and not by name, so wear something comfortable.

- Leave excess paraphernalia at home – Shopping bags and odd bundles will get in your way. You need bring only the items mentioned in the official notice you received; usually everything you need is provided. Do not bring reference books to the exam. They will only confuse those last minutes and be taken away from you when in the test room.
- Arrive somewhat ahead of time – If because of transportation schedules you must get there very early, bring a newspaper or magazine to take your mind off yourself while waiting.
- Locate the examination room – When you have found the proper room, you will be directed to the seat or part of the room where you will sit. Sometimes you are given a sheet of instructions to read while you are waiting. Do not fill out any forms until you are told to do so; just read them and be prepared.
- Relax and prepare to listen to the instructions
- If you have any physical problem that may keep you from doing your best, be sure to tell the test administrator. If you are sick or in poor health, you really cannot do your best on the exam. You can come back and take the test some other time.

## VII. AT THE TEST

The day of the test is here and you have the test booklet in your hand. The temptation to get going is very strong. Caution! There is more to success than knowing the right answers. You must know how to identify your papers and understand variations in the type of short-answer question used in this particular examination. Follow these suggestions for maximum results from your efforts:

### 1) Cooperate with the monitor
The test administrator has a duty to create a situation in which you can be as much at ease as possible. He will give instructions, tell you when to begin, check to see that you are marking your answer sheet correctly, and so on. He is not there to guard you, although he will see that your competitors do not take unfair advantage. He wants to help you do your best.

### 2) Listen to all instructions
Don't jump the gun! Wait until you understand all directions. In most civil service tests you get more time than you need to answer the questions. So don't be in a hurry. Read each word of instructions until you clearly understand the meaning. Study the examples, listen to all announcements and follow directions. Ask questions if you do not understand what to do.

### 3) Identify your papers
Civil service exams are usually identified by number only. You will be assigned a number; you must not put your name on your test papers. Be sure to copy your number correctly. Since more than one exam may be given, copy your exact examination title.

### 4) Plan your time
Unless you are told that a test is a "speed" or "rate of work" test, speed itself is usually not important. Time enough to answer all the questions will be provided, but this does not mean that you have all day. An overall time limit has been set. Divide the total time (in minutes) by the number of questions to determine the approximate time you have for each question.

### 5) Do not linger over difficult questions

If you come across a difficult question, mark it with a paper clip (useful to have along) and come back to it when you have been through the booklet. One caution if you do this – be sure to skip a number on your answer sheet as well. Check often to be sure that you have not lost your place and that you are marking in the row numbered the same as the question you are answering.

### 6) Read the questions

Be sure you know what the question asks! Many capable people are unsuccessful because they failed to *read* the questions correctly.

### 7) Answer all questions

Unless you have been instructed that a penalty will be deducted for incorrect answers, it is better to guess than to omit a question.

### 8) Speed tests

It is often better NOT to guess on speed tests. It has been found that on timed tests people are tempted to spend the last few seconds before time is called in marking answers at random – without even reading them – in the hope of picking up a few extra points. To discourage this practice, the instructions may warn you that your score will be "corrected" for guessing. That is, a penalty will be applied. The incorrect answers will be deducted from the correct ones, or some other penalty formula will be used.

### 9) Review your answers

If you finish before time is called, go back to the questions you guessed or omitted to give them further thought. Review other answers if you have time.

### 10) Return your test materials

If you are ready to leave before others have finished or time is called, take ALL your materials to the monitor and leave quietly. Never take any test material with you. The monitor can discover whose papers are not complete, and taking a test booklet may be grounds for disqualification.


## VIII. EXAMINATION TECHNIQUES

1) Read the general instructions carefully. These are usually printed on the first page of the exam booklet. As a rule, these instructions refer to the timing of the examination; the fact that you should not start work until the signal and must stop work at a signal, etc. If there are any *special* instructions, such as a choice of questions to be answered, make sure that you note this instruction carefully.

2) When you are ready to start work on the examination, that is as soon as the signal has been given, read the instructions to each question booklet, underline any key words or phrases, such as *least, best, outline, describe* and the like. In this way you will tend to answer as requested rather than discover on reviewing your paper that you *listed without describing*, that you selected the *worst* choice rather than the *best* choice, etc.

3) If the examination is of the objective or multiple-choice type – that is, each question will also give a series of possible answers: A, B, C or D, and you are called upon to select the best answer and write the letter next to that answer on your answer paper – it is advisable to start answering each question in turn. There may be anywhere from 50 to 100 such questions in the three or four hours allotted and you can see how much time would be taken if you read through all the questions before beginning to answer any. Furthermore, if you come across a question or group of questions which you know would be difficult to answer, it would undoubtedly affect your handling of all the other questions.

4) If the examination is of the essay type and contains but a few questions, it is a moot point as to whether you should read all the questions before starting to answer any one. Of course, if you are given a choice – say five out of seven and the like – then it is essential to read all the questions so you can eliminate the two that are most difficult. If, however, you are asked to answer all the questions, there may be danger in trying to answer the easiest one first because you may find that you will spend too much time on it. The best technique is to answer the first question, then proceed to the second, etc.

5) Time your answers. Before the exam begins, write down the time it started, then add the time allowed for the examination and write down the time it must be completed, then divide the time available somewhat as follows:
   - If 3-1/2 hours are allowed, that would be 210 minutes. If you have 80 objective-type questions, that would be an average of 2-1/2 minutes per question. Allow yourself no more than 2 minutes per question, or a total of 160 minutes, which will permit about 50 minutes to review.
   - If for the time allotment of 210 minutes there are 7 essay questions to answer, that would average about 30 minutes a question. Give yourself only 25 minutes per question so that you have about 35 minutes to review.

6) The most important instruction is to *read each question* and make sure you know what is wanted. The second most important instruction is to *time yourself properly* so that you answer every question. The third most important instruction is to *answer every question.* Guess if you have to but include something for each question. Remember that you will receive no credit for a blank and will probably receive some credit if you write something in answer to an essay question. If you guess a letter – say "B" for a multiple-choice question – you may have guessed right. If you leave a blank as an answer to a multiple-choice question, the examiners may respect your feelings but it will not add a point to your score. Some exams may penalize you for wrong answers, so in such cases *only*, you may not want to guess unless you have some basis for your answer.

7) Suggestions
   a. Objective-type questions
      1. Examine the question booklet for proper sequence of pages and questions
      2. Read all instructions carefully
      3. Skip any question which seems too difficult; return to it after all other questions have been answered
      4. Apportion your time properly; do not spend too much time on any single question or group of questions

5. Note and underline key words – *all, most, fewest, least, best, worst, same, opposite*, etc.
6. Pay particular attention to negatives
7. Note unusual option, e.g., unduly long, short, complex, different or similar in content to the body of the question
8. Observe the use of "hedging" words – *probably, may, most likely*, etc.
9. Make sure that your answer is put next to the same number as the question
10. Do not second-guess unless you have good reason to believe the second answer is definitely more correct
11. Cross out original answer if you decide another answer is more accurate; do not erase until you are ready to hand your paper in
12. Answer all questions; guess unless instructed otherwise
13. Leave time for review

   b. Essay questions
   1. Read each question carefully
   2. Determine exactly what is wanted. Underline key words or phrases.
   3. Decide on outline or paragraph answer
   4. Include many different points and elements unless asked to develop any one or two points or elements
   5. Show impartiality by giving pros and cons unless directed to select one side only
   6. Make and write down any assumptions you find necessary to answer the questions
   7. Watch your English, grammar, punctuation and choice of words
   8. Time your answers; don't crowd material

8) Answering the essay question

Most essay questions can be answered by framing the specific response around several key words or ideas. Here are a few such key words or ideas:

M's: manpower, materials, methods, money, management
P's: purpose, program, policy, plan, procedure, practice, problems, pitfalls, personnel, public relations
   a. Six basic steps in handling problems:
   1. Preliminary plan and background development
   2. Collect information, data and facts
   3. Analyze and interpret information, data and facts
   4. Analyze and develop solutions as well as make recommendations
   5. Prepare report and sell recommendations
   6. Install recommendations and follow up effectiveness

   b. Pitfalls to avoid
   1. *Taking things for granted* – A statement of the situation does not necessarily imply that each of the elements is necessarily true; for example, a complaint may be invalid and biased so that all that can be taken for granted is that a complaint has been registered

2. *Considering only one side of a situation* – Wherever possible, indicate several alternatives and then point out the reasons you selected the best one
3. *Failing to indicate follow up* – Whenever your answer indicates action on your part, make certain that you will take proper follow-up action to see how successful your recommendations, procedures or actions turn out to be
4. *Taking too long in answering any single question* – Remember to time your answers properly

## IX. AFTER THE TEST

Scoring procedures differ in detail among civil service jurisdictions although the general principles are the same. Whether the papers are hand-scored or graded by machine we have described, they are nearly always graded by number. That is, the person who marks the paper knows only the number – never the name – of the applicant. Not until all the papers have been graded will they be matched with names. If other tests, such as training and experience or oral interview ratings have been given, scores will be combined. Different parts of the examination usually have different weights. For example, the written test might count 60 percent of the final grade, and a rating of training and experience 40 percent. In many jurisdictions, veterans will have a certain number of points added to their grades.

After the final grade has been determined, the names are placed in grade order and an eligible list is established. There are various methods for resolving ties between those who get the same final grade – probably the most common is to place first the name of the person whose application was received first. Job offers are made from the eligible list in the order the names appear on it. You will be notified of your grade and your rank as soon as all these computations have been made. This will be done as rapidly as possible.

People who are found to meet the requirements in the announcement are called "eligibles." Their names are put on a list of eligible candidates. An eligible's chances of getting a job depend on how high he stands on this list and how fast agencies are filling jobs from the list.

When a job is to be filled from a list of eligibles, the agency asks for the names of people on the list of eligibles for that job. When the civil service commission receives this request, it sends to the agency the names of the three people highest on this list. Or, if the job to be filled has specialized requirements, the office sends the agency the names of the top three persons who meet these requirements from the general list.

The appointing officer makes a choice from among the three people whose names were sent to him. If the selected person accepts the appointment, the names of the others are put back on the list to be considered for future openings.

That is the rule in hiring from all kinds of eligible lists, whether they are for typist, carpenter, chemist, or something else. For every vacancy, the appointing officer has his choice of any one of the top three eligibles on the list. This explains why the person whose name is on top of the list sometimes does not get an appointment when some of the persons lower on the list do. If the appointing officer chooses the second or third eligible, the No. 1 eligible does not get a job at once, but stays on the list until he is appointed or the list is terminated.

## X. HOW TO PASS THE INTERVIEW TEST

The examination for which you applied requires an oral interview test. You have already taken the written test and you are now being called for the interview test – the final part of the formal examination.

You may think that it is not possible to prepare for an interview test and that there are no procedures to follow during an interview. Our purpose is to point out some things you can do in advance that will help you and some good rules to follow and pitfalls to avoid while you are being interviewed.

### What is an interview supposed to test?

The written examination is designed to test the technical knowledge and competence of the candidate; the oral is designed to evaluate intangible qualities, not readily measured otherwise, and to establish a list showing the relative fitness of each candidate – as measured against his competitors – for the position sought. Scoring is not on the basis of "right" and "wrong," but on a sliding scale of values ranging from "not passable" to "outstanding." As a matter of fact, it is possible to achieve a relatively low score without a single "incorrect" answer because of evident weakness in the qualities being measured.

Occasionally, an examination may consist entirely of an oral test – either an individual or a group oral. In such cases, information is sought concerning the technical knowledges and abilities of the candidate, since there has been no written examination for this purpose. More commonly, however, an oral test is used to supplement a written examination.

### Who conducts interviews?

The composition of oral boards varies among different jurisdictions. In nearly all, a representative of the personnel department serves as chairman. One of the members of the board may be a representative of the department in which the candidate would work. In some cases, "outside experts" are used, and, frequently, a businessman or some other representative of the general public is asked to serve. Labor and management or other special groups may be represented. The aim is to secure the services of experts in the appropriate field.

However the board is composed, it is a good idea (and not at all improper or unethical) to ascertain in advance of the interview who the members are and what groups they represent. When you are introduced to them, you will have some idea of their backgrounds and interests, and at least you will not stutter and stammer over their names.

### What should be done before the interview?

While knowledge about the board members is useful and takes some of the surprise element out of the interview, there is other preparation which is more substantive. It *is* possible to prepare for an oral interview – in several ways:

### 1) Keep a copy of your application and review it carefully before the interview

This may be the only document before the oral board, and the starting point of the interview. Know what education and experience you have listed there, and the sequence and dates of all of it. Sometimes the board will ask you to review the highlights of your experience for them; you should not have to hem and haw doing it.

### 2) Study the class specification and the examination announcement

Usually, the oral board has one or both of these to guide them. The qualities, characteristics or knowledges required by the position sought are stated in these documents. They offer valuable clues as to the nature of the oral interview. For example, if the job involves supervisory responsibilities, the announcement will usually indicate that knowledge of modern supervisory methods and the qualifications of the candidate as a supervisor will be tested. If so, you can expect such questions, frequently in the form of a hypothetical situation which you are expected to solve. NEVER go into an oral without knowledge of the duties and responsibilities of the job you seek.

### 3) Think through each qualification required

Try to visualize the kind of questions you would ask if you were a board member. How well could you answer them? Try especially to appraise your own knowledge and background in each area, *measured against the job sought,* and identify any areas in which you are weak. Be critical and realistic – do not flatter yourself.

### 4) Do some general reading in areas in which you feel you may be weak

For example, if the job involves supervision and your past experience has NOT, some general reading in supervisory methods and practices, particularly in the field of human relations, might be useful. Do NOT study agency procedures or detailed manuals. The oral board will be testing your understanding and capacity, not your memory.

### 5) Get a good night's sleep and watch your general health and mental attitude

You will want a clear head at the interview. Take care of a cold or any other minor ailment, and of course, no hangovers.

*What should be done on the day of the interview?*

Now comes the day of the interview itself. Give yourself plenty of time to get there. Plan to arrive somewhat ahead of the scheduled time, particularly if your appointment is in the fore part of the day. If a previous candidate fails to appear, the board might be ready for you a bit early. By early afternoon an oral board is almost invariably behind schedule if there are many candidates, and you may have to wait. Take along a book or magazine to read, or your application to review, but leave any extraneous material in the waiting room when you go in for your interview. In any event, relax and compose yourself.

The matter of dress is important. The board is forming impressions about you – from your experience, your manners, your attitude, and your appearance. Give your personal appearance careful attention. Dress your best, but not your flashiest. Choose conservative, appropriate clothing, and be sure it is immaculate. This is a business interview, and your appearance should indicate that you regard it as such. Besides, being well groomed and properly dressed will help boost your confidence.

Sooner or later, someone will call your name and escort you into the interview room. *This is it.* From here on you are on your own. It is too late for any more preparation. But remember, you asked for this opportunity to prove your fitness, and you are here because your request was granted.

*What happens when you go in?*

The usual sequence of events will be as follows: The clerk (who is often the board stenographer) will introduce you to the chairman of the oral board, who will introduce you to the other members of the board. Acknowledge the introductions before you sit down. Do not be surprised if you find a microphone facing you or a stenotypist sitting by. Oral interviews are usually recorded in the event of an appeal or other review.

Usually the chairman of the board will open the interview by reviewing the highlights of your education and work experience from your application – primarily for the benefit of the other members of the board, as well as to get the material into the record. Do not interrupt or comment unless there is an error or significant misinterpretation; if that is the case, do not hesitate. But do not quibble about insignificant matters. Also, he will usually ask you some question about your education, experience or your present job – partly to get you to start talking and to establish the interviewing "rapport." He may start the actual questioning, or turn it over to one of the other members. Frequently, each member undertakes the questioning on a particular area, one in which he is perhaps most competent, so you can expect each member to participate in the examination. Because time is limited, you may also expect some rather abrupt switches in the direction the questioning takes, so do not be upset by it. Normally, a board member will not pursue a single line of questioning unless he discovers a particular strength or weakness.

After each member has participated, the chairman will usually ask whether any member has any further questions, then will ask you if you have anything you wish to add. Unless you are expecting this question, it may floor you. Worse, it may start you off on an extended, extemporaneous speech. The board is not usually seeking more information. The question is principally to offer you a last opportunity to present further qualifications or to indicate that you have nothing to add. So, if you feel that a significant qualification or characteristic has been overlooked, it is proper to point it out in a sentence or so. Do not compliment the board on the thoroughness of their examination – they have been sketchy, and you know it. If you wish, merely say, "No thank you, I have nothing further to add." This is a point where you can "talk yourself out" of a good impression or fail to present an important bit of information. Remember, *you close the interview yourself.*

The chairman will then say, "That is all, Mr. _____, thank you." Do not be startled; the interview is over, and quicker than you think. Thank him, gather your belongings and take your leave. Save your sigh of relief for the other side of the door.


*How to put your best foot forward*
Throughout this entire process, you may feel that the board individually and collectively is trying to pierce your defenses, seek out your hidden weaknesses and embarrass and confuse you. Actually, this is not true. They are obliged to make an appraisal of your qualifications for the job you are seeking, and they want to see you in your best light. Remember, they must interview all candidates and a non-cooperative candidate may become a failure in spite of their best efforts to bring out his qualifications. Here are 15 suggestions that will help you:

**1) Be natural – Keep your attitude confident, not cocky**
If you are not confident that you can do the job, do not expect the board to be. Do not apologize for your weaknesses, try to bring out your strong points. The board is interested in a positive, not negative, presentation. Cockiness will antagonize any board member and make him wonder if you are covering up a weakness by a false show of strength.

**2) Get comfortable, but don't lounge or sprawl**
Sit erectly but not stiffly. A careless posture may lead the board to conclude that you are careless in other things, or at least that you are not impressed by the importance of the occasion. Either conclusion is natural, even if incorrect. Do not fuss with your clothing, a pencil or an ashtray. Your hands may occasionally be useful to emphasize a point; do not let them become a point of distraction.

**3) Do not wisecrack or make small talk**
This is a serious situation, and your attitude should show that you consider it as such. Further, the time of the board is limited – they do not want to waste it, and neither should you.

## 4) Do not exaggerate your experience or abilities

In the first place, from information in the application or other interviews and sources, the board may know more about you than you think. Secondly, you probably will not get away with it. An experienced board is rather adept at spotting such a situation, so do not take the chance.

## 5) If you know a board member, do not make a point of it, yet do not hide it

Certainly you are not fooling him, and probably not the other members of the board. Do not try to take advantage of your acquaintanceship – it will probably do you little good.

## 6) Do not dominate the interview

Let the board do that. They will give you the clues – do not assume that you have to do all the talking. Realize that the board has a number of questions to ask you, and do not try to take up all the interview time by showing off your extensive knowledge of the answer to the first one.

## 7) Be attentive

You only have 20 minutes or so, and you should keep your attention at its sharpest throughout. When a member is addressing a problem or question to you, give him your undivided attention. Address your reply principally to him, but do not exclude the other board members.

## 8) Do not interrupt

A board member may be stating a problem for you to analyze. He will ask you a question when the time comes. Let him state the problem, and wait for the question.

## 9) Make sure you understand the question

Do not try to answer until you are sure what the question is. If it is not clear, restate it in your own words or ask the board member to clarify it for you. However, do not haggle about minor elements.

## 10) Reply promptly but not hastily

A common entry on oral board rating sheets is "candidate responded readily," or "candidate hesitated in replies." Respond as promptly and quickly as you can, but do not jump to a hasty, ill-considered answer.

## 11) Do not be peremptory in your answers

A brief answer is proper – but do not fire your answer back. That is a losing game from your point of view. The board member can probably ask questions much faster than you can answer them.

## 12) Do not try to create the answer you think the board member wants

He is interested in what kind of mind you have and how it works – not in playing games. Furthermore, he can usually spot this practice and will actually grade you down on it.

## 13) Do not switch sides in your reply merely to agree with a board member

Frequently, a member will take a contrary position merely to draw you out and to see if you are willing and able to defend your point of view. Do not start a debate, yet do not surrender a good position. If a position is worth taking, it is worth defending.

**14) Do not be afraid to admit an error in judgment if you are shown to be wrong**

The board knows that you are forced to reply without any opportunity for careful consideration. Your answer may be demonstrably wrong. If so, admit it and get on with the interview.

**15) Do not dwell at length on your present job**

The opening question may relate to your present assignment. Answer the question but do not go into an extended discussion. You are being examined for a *new* job, not your present one. As a matter of fact, try to phrase ALL your answers in terms of the job for which you are being examined.

*Basis of Rating*

Probably you will forget most of these "do's" and "don'ts" when you walk into the oral interview room. Even remembering them all will not ensure you a passing grade. Perhaps you did not have the qualifications in the first place. But remembering them will help you to put your best foot forward, without treading on the toes of the board members.

Rumor and popular opinion to the contrary notwithstanding, an oral board wants you to make the best appearance possible. They know you are under pressure – but they also want to see how you respond to it as a guide to what your reaction would be under the pressures of the job you seek. They will be influenced by the degree of poise you display, the personal traits you show and the manner in which you respond.


ABOUT THIS BOOK

This book contains tests divided into Examination Sections. Go through each test, answering every question in the margin. We have also attached a sample answer sheet at the back of the book that can be removed and used. At the end of each test look at the answer key and check your answers. On the ones you got wrong, look at the right answer choice and learn. Do not fill in the answers first. Do not memorize the questions and answers, but understand the answer and principles involved. On your test, the questions will likely be different from the samples. Questions are changed and new ones added. If you understand these past questions you should have success with any changes that arise. Tests may consist of several types of questions. We have additional books on each subject should more study be advisable or necessary for you. Finally, the more you study, the better prepared you will be. This book is intended to be the last thing you study before you walk into the examination room. Prior study of relevant texts is also recommended. NLC publishes some of these in our Fundamental Series. Knowledge and good sense are important factors in passing your exam. Good luck also helps. So now study this Passbook, absorb the material contained within and take that knowledge into the examination. Then do your best to pass that exam.

# EXAMINATION SECTION

# EXAMINATION SECTION

# TEST 1

DIRECTIONS: Each question or incomplete statement is followed by several suggested answers or completions. Select the one that BEST answers the question or completes the statement. *PRINT THE LETTER OF THE CORRECT ANSWER IN THE SPACE AT THE RIGHT.*

Questions 1-5.

DIRECTIONS: Questions 1 through 5 are to be answered on the basis of the extracts from Federal income tax withholding and Social Security tax tables shown below. These tables indicate the amounts which must be withheld from the employee's salary by his employer for Federal income tax and for Social Security. They are based on weekly earnings.

| INCOME TAX WITHHOLDING TABLE | | | | | | | |
|---|---|---|---|---|---|---|---|
| The wages are | | And the number of withholding allowances is | | | | | |
| At Least | But Less Than | 5 | 6 | 7 | 8 | 9 | 10 or More |
| | | The amount of income tax to be withheld shall be | | | | | |
| $300 | $320 | $24.60 | $19.00 | $13.80 | $ 8.60 | $4.00 | $ 0 |
| 320 | 340 | 28.80 | 22.80 | 17.40 | 12.20 | 7.00 | 2.80 |
| 340 | 360 | 33.00 | 27.00 | 21.00 | 15.80 | 10.60 | 5.60 |
| 360 | 380 | 37.20 | 31.20 | 25.20 | 19.40 | 14.20 | 9.00 |
| 380 | 400 | 41.40 | 34.40 | 29.40 | 23.40 | 17.80 | 12.60 |
| 400 | 420 | 45.60 | 39.60 | 33.60 | 27.60 | 21.40 | 16.20 |
| 420 | 440 | 49.80 | 43.80 | 37.80 | 31.80 | 25.60 | 19.80 |
| 440 | 460 | 54.00 | 48.00 | 42.00 | 36.00 | 29.80 | 23.80 |
| 460 | 480 | 58.20 | 52.20 | 46.20 | 40.20 | 34.00 | 38.00 |
| 480 | 500 | 62.40 | 46.40 | 40.40 | 44.40 | 38.20 | 32.20 |

| SOCIAL SECURITY TABLE | | | | | |
|---|---|---|---|---|---|
| WAGES | | | WAGES | | |
| At Least | But Less Than | Tax to be Withheld | At Least | But Less Than | Tax to be Withheld |
| $333.18 | $333.52 | $19.50 | $336.60 | $336.94 | $19.70 |
| 333.52 | 333.86 | 19.52 | 336.94 | 337.28 | 19.72 |
| 333.86 | 334.20 | 19.54 | 337.28 | 337.62 | 19.74 |
| 334.20 | 334.54 | 19.56 | 337.62 | 337.96 | 19.76 |
| 334.54 | 334.88 | 19.58 | 337.96 | 338.30 | 19.78 |
| 334.88 | 335.22 | 19.60 | 338.30 | 338.64 | 19.80 |
| 335.22 | 335.56 | 19.62 | 338.64 | 338.98 | 19.82 |
| 335.56 | 335.90 | 19.64 | 338.98 | 339.32 | 19.84 |
| 335.90 | 336.24 | 19.66 | 339.32 | 339.66 | 19.86 |
| 336.24 | 336.60 | 19.68 | 339.66 | 340.00 | 19.88 |

1.  If an employee has a weekly wage of $379.50 and claims 6 withholding      1.____
    allowances, the amount of income tax to be withheld is
       A.  $27.00     B.  $31.20     C.  $35.40     D.  $37.20

2.  An employee had wages of $335.60 for one week.      2.____
    With eight withholding allowances claimed, how much income tax will be
    withheld from his salary?
       A.  $8.60     B.  $12.00     C.  $13.80     D.  $17.40

3.  How much social security tax will an employee with weekly wages of $335.60      3.____
    pay?
       A.  $19.60     B.  $19.62     C.  $19.64     D.  $19.66

4.  Mr. Wise earns $339.80 a week and claims seven withholding allowances.      4.____
    What is his take-home pay after income tax and social security tax are deducted?
       A.  $300.32     B.  $302.52     C.  $319.92     D.  $322.40

5.  If an employee pays $19.74 in social security tax and claims eight withholding      5.____
    allowances, the amount of income tax that should be withheld from his wages is
       A.  $8.60     B.  $12.20     C.  $13.80     D.  $15.80

6.  A fundamental rule of bookkeeping states that an individual's assets equal his      6.____
    liabilities plus his proprietorship (ASSETS = LIABILITIES – PROPRIETORSHIP).
    Which of the following statements logically follows from this rule?
       A.  ASSETS = PROPRIETORSHIP – LIABILITIES
       B.  LIABILITIES = ASSETS + PROPRIETORSHIP
       C.  PROPRIETORSHIP = ASSETS – LIABILITIES
       D.  PROPRIETORSHIP = LIABILITIES + ASSETS

7.  Mr. Martin's assets consist of the following:      7.____
       Cash on Hand:     $5,233.74
       Furniture:     $4,925.00
       Government Bonds:   $5,500.00
    What are his TOTAL assets?
       A.  $10,158.74     $10,425.00     C.  $10,733.74     D.  $15,658.74

8.  If Mr. Mitchell has $627.04 in his checking account and then writes three checks      8.____
    for $241.74, $13.24, and $101.97, what will be his new balance?
       A.  $257.88     B.  $269.08     C.  $357.96     D.  $368.96

9.  An employee's net pay is equal to his total earnings less all deductions.      9.____
    If an employee's total earnings in a pay period are $497.05, what is his NET pay
    if he has the following deductions:  Federal income tax, $90.32; FICA: $28.74;
    State tax: $18.79; City tax: $7.25; Pension: $1.88?
       A.  $351.17     B.  $351.07     C.  $350.17     D.  $350.07

10. A petty cash fund had an opening balance of $85.75 on December 1.      10._____
Expenditures of $23.00, $15.65, $5.23, $14.75, and $26.38 were made out of his
fund during the first 14 days of the month.  Then, on December 17, another
$38.50 was added to the fund.
If additional expenditures of $17.18, $3.29, and $11.64 were made during the
remainder of the month, what was the FINAL balance of the petty cash fund at
the end of December?
   A.  $6.93       B.  $7.13       C.  $46.51       D.  $91.40

Questions 11-15.

DIRECTIONS:   Questions 11 through 15 are to be answered on the basis of the following
instructions.

The chart below is used by the loan division of a city retirement system for the following
purposes:  (1) to calculate the monthly payment a member must pay on an outstanding loan; (2)
to calculate how much a member owes on an outstanding loan after he has made a number of
payments.

To calculate the amount a member must pay each month in repaying his loan, look at
Column II on the chart.  You will notice that each entry in Column II corresponds to a number
appearing under the *Months* column; for example, 1.004868 corresponds to 1 month, 0.503654
corresponds to 2 months, etc.  To calculate the amount a member must pay each month, use
the following procedure:  multiply the amount of the load by the entry in Column II which
corresponds to the number of months over which the load will be paid back.  For example, if a
loan of $200 is taken out for six months, multiply $200 by 0.169518, the entry in Column II which
corresponds to six months.

In order to calculate the balance still owed on an outstanding loan, multiply the monthly
payment by the number in Column I which corresponds to the number of monthly payments
which remain to be paid on the loan.  For example, if a member is supposed to pay $106.00 a
month for twelve months, after seven payments, five monthly payments remain.  To calculate
the balance owed on the loan at this point, multiply the $106.00 monthly payment by 4.927807,
the number in Column I that corresponds to five months.

| Months | Column I | Column II |
|--------|----------|-----------|
| 1 | 0.995156 | 1.004868 |
| 2 | 1.985491 | 0.503654 |
| 3 | 2.971029 | 0.336584 |
| 4 | 3.951793 | 0.253050 |
| 5 | 4.927807 | 0.202930 |
| 6 | 5.899092 | 0.169518 |
| 7 | 6.865673 | 0.145652 |
| 8 | 7.827572 | 0.127754 |
| 9 | 8.784811 | 0.113833 |
| 10 | 9.737414 | 0.102697 |
| 11 | 10.685402 | 0.093586 |
| 12 | 11.628798 | 0.085994 |
| 13 | 12.567624 | 0.079570 |
| 14 | 13.501902 | 0.074064 |
| 15 | 14.431655 | 0.069292 |

11. If Mr. Carson borrows $1,500 for eight months, how much will he have to pay back each month?     11.____
    A. $187.16      B. $191.63      C. $208.72      D. $218.65

12. If a member borrows $2,400 for one year, the amount he will have to pay back each month is    12.____
    A. $118.78      B. $196.18      C. $202.28      D. $206.38

13. Mr. Elliott borrowed $1,700 for a period of fifteen months.
Each month he will have to pay back    13.____
    A. $117.80      B. $116.96      C. $107.79      D. $101.79

14. Mr. Aylward is paying back a thirteen-month loan at the rate of $173.13 a month.
If he has already made six monthly payments, how much does he owe on the outstanding loan?    14.____
    A. $1,027.38      B. $1,178.75      C. $1,188.65      D. $1,898.85

15. A loan was taken out for 15 months, and the monthly payment was $104.75. After two monthly payments, how much was still owed on this load?    15.____
    A. $515.79      B. $863.89      C. $1,116.76      D. $1,316.46

16. The ABC Corporation had a gross income of $125,500.00 in 2015. Of this, it paid 60% for overhead.    16.____
If the gross income for 2016 increased by $6,500 and the cost of overhead increased to 61% of gross income, how much more did it pay for overhead in 2016 than in 2015?
    A. $1,320      B. $5,220      C. $7,530      D. $8,052

17. After one year, Mr. Richards paid back a total of $1,695.00 as payment for    17.____
a $1,500.00 loan. All the money paid over $1,500.00 was simple interest.
The interest charge was MOST NEARLY
   A. 13%     B. 11%     C. 9%     D. 7%

18. A checking account has a balance of $253.36.    18.____
If deposits of $36.95, $210.23, and $7.34 and withdrawals of $117.35, $23.37,
and $15.98 are made, what is the NEW balance of the account?
   A. $155.54     B. $351.18     C. $364.58     D. $664.58

19. In 2015, the W Realty Company spent 27% of its income on rent.    19.____
If it earned $97,254.00 in 2015, the amount it paid for rent was
   A. $26.258.58     B. $26,348.58     C. $27,248.58     D. $27,358.58

20. Six percent simple annual interest on $2,436.18 is MOST NEARLY    20.____
   A. $145.08     B. $145.17     c. $146.08     D. $146.17

21. Assume that the XYZ Company has $10,402.72 cash on hand.    21.____
If it pays $699.83 of this for rent, the amount of cash on hand would be
   A. $9,792.89     B. $9,702.89     C. $9,692.89     D. $9,602.89

22. On January 31, Mr. Warren's checking account had a balance of $933.68.    22.____
If he deposited $36.40 on February 2, $126.00 on February 9, and $90.02 on
February 16 and wrote no checks during this period, what was the balance of his
account on February 17?
   A. $680.26     B. $681.26     C. $1,186.10     D. $1,187.00

23. Multiplying a number by .75 is the same as    23.____
   A. multiplying it by 2/3     B. dividing it by 2/3
   C. multiplying it by 3/4     D. dividing it by 3/4

24. In City Agency A, 2/3 of the employees are enrolled in a retirement system.    24.____
City Agency B has the same number of employees as Agency A, and 60% of
these are enrolled in a retirement system.
If Agency A has a total of 660 employees, how many MORE employees does it
have enrolled in a retirement system than does Agency B?
   B. 36     B. 44     C. 56     D. 66

25. Net Worth is equal to Assets minus Liabilities.    25.____
If, at the end of year, a textile company had assets of $98,695.83 and liabilities of
$59,238.29, what was its net worth?
   A. $38,478.54     B. $38,488.64     C. $39,457.54     D. $48,557.54

# KEY (CORRECT ANSWERS)

| | | | | |
|---|---|---|---|---|
| 1. | B | | 11. | B |
| 2. | B | | 12. | D |
| 3. | C | | 13. | A |
| 4. | B | | 14. | C |
| 5. | B | | 15. | D |
| | | | | |
| 6. | C | | 16. | B |
| 7. | D | | 17. | A |
| 8. | B | | 18. | B |
| 9. | D | | 19. | A |
| 10. | B | | 20. | D |

| | |
|---|---|
| 21. | B |
| 22. | C |
| 23. | C |
| 24. | B |
| 25. | C |

———

# TEST 2

DIRECTIONS: Each question or incomplete statement is followed by several suggested answers or completions. Select the one that BEST answers the question or completes the statement. *PRINT THE LETTER OF THE CORRECT ANSWER IN THE SPACE AT THE RIGHT.*

Questions 1-10.

DIRECTIONS: Questions 1 through 10 below present the identification numbers, initials, and last names of employees enrolled in a city retirement system. You are to choose the option (A, B, C, or D) that has the IDENTICAL identification number, initials, and last name as those given in each question.

Sample Question
B145698 JL Jones
    A.    B146798 JL Jones           B.  B145698 JL Jonas
    C.    P145698 JL Jones           D. B145698 JL Jones

The correct answer is D. Only Option D shows the identification number, initials, and last name exactly as they are in the sample question. Options A, B, and C have errors in the identification number or last name.

1.    J297483 PL Robinson                                  1.\_\_\_\_
    A. J294783 PL Robinson         B. J297483 PL Robinson
    C. J297483 PI Robinson          D. J297843 PL Robinson

2.    S497662 JG Schwartz                                  2.\_\_\_\_
    B.    S497662 JG Schwarz       B. S497762 JG Schwartz
    C.    S497662 JG Schwartz      D. S497663 JG Schwartz

3.    G696436 LN Alberton                                  3.\_\_\_\_
    A. G696436 LM Alberton       B. G696436 LN Albertson
    C. G696346 LN Albertson      D. G696436 LN Alberton

4.    R774923 AD Aldrich                                  4.\_\_\_\_
    A. R774923 AD Aldrich        B. R744923 AD Aldrich
    C. R774932 AP Aldrich        D. R774932 AD Allrich

5.    N239638 RP Hrynyk                                  5.\_\_\_\_
    A. N236938 PR Hrynyk        B. N236938 RP Hrynyk
    C. N239638 PR Hrynyk        D. N239638 Hrynyk

6.    R156949 LT Carlson                                  6.\_\_\_\_
    A. R156949 LT Carlton        B. R156494 LT Carlson
    C. R159649 LT Carlton        D. R156949 LT Carlson

7.    T524697 MN Orenstein                                7.\_\_\_\_
    A. T524697 MN Orenstein      B. T524967 MN Orinstein
    C. T524697 NM Ornstein       D. T524967 NM Orenstein

8.  L346239 JD Remsen                                                    8._____
    A.  L346239 JD Remson          B.  L364239 JD Remsen
    C.  L346329 JD Remsen          D.  L346239 JD Remsen

9.  P966438 SB Rieperson                                                 9._____
    A.  P996438 SB Rieperson       B.  P466438 SB Reiperson
    C.  R996438 SB Rieperson       D.  P966438 SB Rieperson

10. D749382 CD Thompson                                                  10._____
    A.  P749382 CD Thompson        B.  D749832 CD Thomsonn
    C.  D749382 CD Thompson        D.  D749823 CD Thomspon

Questions 11-20.

DIRECTIONS:  Assume that each of the capital letters in the table below represents the name
of an employee enrolled in the city's employees' personnel system.  The
number directly beneath the letter represents the agency for which the
employee works, and the small letter directly beneath represents the code for
the employee's account.

| Name of Employee | L | O | T | Q | A | M | R | N | C |
|---|---|---|---|---|---|---|---|---|---|
| Agency | 3 | 4 | 5 | 9 | 8 | 7 | 2 | 1 | 6 |
| Account Code | r | f | b | i | d | t | g | e | n |

In each of the following Questions 11 through 20, the agency code numbers
and the account code letters in Columns 2 and 3 should correspond to the
capital letters in Column 1 and should be in the same consecutive order.  For
each question, look at each column carefully and mark your answer as follows:

If there are one or more errors in Column 2 only, mark your answer A.
If there are one or more errors in Column 3 only, mark your answer B.
I there are one or more errors in Column 2 and one or more errors in Column 3,
mark your answer C.
If there are NO errors in either column, mark your answer D.

Sample Question

Column 1     Column 2     Column 3
TQLMOC       583746       birtfn

In Column 2, the second agency code number (corresponding to letter Q)
should be 9, not 8.  Column 3 is coded correctly to Column 1.  Since there is an
error only in Column 2, the correct answer is A.

| | COLUMN 1 | COLUMN 2 | COLUMN 3 | |
|---|---|---|---|---|
| 11. | QLNRCA | 931268 | iregnd | 11._____ |
| 12. | NRMOTC | 127546 | egftbn | 12._____ |
| 13. | RCTALM | 265837 | gndbrt | 13._____ |
| 14. | TAMLON | 578341 | bdtrfe | 14._____ |
| 15. | ANTORM | 815427 | debigt | 15._____ |
| 16. | MRALON | 728341 | tgdrfe | 16._____ |
| 17. | CTNQRO | 657924 | ndeigf | 17._____ |
| 18. | QMROTA | 972458 | itgfbd | 18._____ |
| 19. | RQMCOL | 297463 | gitnfr | 19._____ |
| 20. | NOMRTQ | 147259 | eftgbi | 20._____ |

Questions 21-25.

DIRECTIONS: Questions 21 through 25 are to be answered SOLELY on the basis of the following passage.

The city may issue its own bonds or it may purchase bonds as an investment. Bonds may be issued in various denominations, and the face value of the bond is its par value. Before purchasing a bond, the investor desires to know the rate of income that the investment may yield in computing the yield on a bond, it is assumed that the investor will keep the bond until the date of maturity, except for callable bonds which are not considered in this passage. To compute exact yield is a complicated mathematical problem, and scientifically prepared tables are generally used to avoid such computation. However, the approximate yield can be computed much more easily. In computing approximate yield, the accrued interest on the date of purchase should be ignored because the buyer who pays accrued interest to the seller receives it again at the next interest date. Bonds bought at a premium (which cost more) yield a lower rate of income than the same bonds bought at par (face value), and bounds bought at a discount (which cost less) yield a higher rate of income than the same bonds bought at par.

21. An investor bought a $10,000 city bond paying 6% interest. Which of the following purchase prices would indicate that the bond was bought at a premium? 21._____
   A. $9,000   B. $9,400   C. $10,000   D. $10,600

22. During 2016, a particular $10,000 bond paying 7 ½% sold at fluctuating prices. Which of the following prices would indicate that the bond was bought at a discount? 22._____
   A. $9,800   B. $10,000   C. $10,200   D. $10,750

23. A certain group of bonds was sold in denominations of $5,000, $10,000,     23.____
$20,000, and $50,000.
In the following list of four purchase prices, which one is MOST likely to represent
a bond sold at par value?
   A. $10,500      B. $20,000      C. $22,000    D. $49,000

24. When computing the approximate yield on a bond, it is DESIRABLE to     24.____
   A. assume the bond was purchased at par
   B. consult scientifically prepared tables
   C. ignore accrued interest on the date of purchase
   D. wait until the bond reaches maturity

25. Which of the following is MOST likely to be an exception to the information     25.____
provided in the above passage?
Bonds
   A. purchased at a premium      B. sold at par
   C. sold before maturity        D. which are callable

_____

# KEY (CORRECT ANSWERS)

| | | | | |
|---|---|---|---|---|
| 1. | B | | 11. | D |
| 2. | C | | 12. | C |
| 3. | D | | 13. | B |
| 4. | A | | 14. | A |
| 5. | D | | 15. | B |
| | | | | |
| 6. | D | | 16. | D |
| 7. | A | | 17. | C |
| 8. | D | | 18. | D |
| 9. | D | | 19. | A |
| 10. | C | | 20. | D |

| | |
|---|---|
| 21. | D |
| 22. | A |
| 23. | B |
| 24. | C |
| 25. | D |

_____

# TEST 3

DIRECTIONS: Each question or incomplete statement is followed by several suggested answers or completions. Select the one that BEST answers the question or completes the statement. *PRINT THE LETTER OF THE CORRECT ANSWER IN THE SPACE AT THE RIGHT.*

Questions 1-6.

DIRECTIONS: Questions 1 through 6 consist of computations of addition, subtraction, multiplication, and division. For each question, do the computation indicated, and choose the correct answer from the four choices given.

1. ADD:  8936
        7821
        8953
        4297
        9785
        6579

   A. 45371      B. 45381      C. 46371      D. 46381      1._____

2. SUBTRACT:  95,432
             67,596

   A. 27,836     B. 27,846     C. 27,936     D. 27,946     2._____

3. MULTIPLY:  987
             867

   A. 854609    B. 854729    C. 855709    D. 855729       3._____

4. DIVIDE:  59)321439.0

   A. 5438.1     B. 5447.1     C. 5448.1     D. 5457.1     4._____

5. DIVIDE:  .057)721

   A. 12,648.0   B. 12,648.1   C. 12,649.0   D. 12,649.1   5._____

6. ADD:  1/2 + 5/7
   A. 1 3/14     B. 1 2/7      C. 1 5/14     D. 1 3/7       6._____

7. If the total number of employees in one city agency increased from 1,927 to 2,006 during a certain year, the percentage increase in the number of employees for that year is MOST NEARLY
   A. 4%         B. 5%         C. 6%         D. 7%          7._____

8.  During a single fiscal year, which totaled 248 workdays, one account clerk          8.____
    verified 1,488 purchase vouchers.
    Assuming a normal work week of five days, what is the average number of
    vouchers verified by the account clerk in a one-week period during this fiscal
    year?
    A.  25                  B.  30                  C.  35                  D.  40

9.  If the city department of purchase bought 190 computers for $793.50 each and     9.____
    208 computers for $839.90 each, the TOTAL price paid for these computers is
    A.  $315,813.00                    B.  $325,464.20
    C.  $334,279.20                    D.  $335,863.00

Questions 10-14.

DIRECTIONS:    Questions 10 through 14 are to be answered SOLELY on the basis of the
               information given in the following paragraph.

Since discounts are in common use in the commercial world and apply to purchases made
by government agencies as well as business firms, it is essential that individuals in both public
and private employment who prepare bills, check invoices, prepare payment vouchers, or write
checks to pay bills have an understanding of the terms used.  These include cash or time
discount, trade discount, and disconnect series.  A cash or time discount offers a reduction in
price to the buyer for the prompt payment of the bill and is usually expressed as a percentage
with a time requirement, stated in days, within which the bill must be paid in order to earn the
discount.  An example would be 3/10, meaning a 3% discount may be applied to the bill if the
payment is forwarded to the vendor within ten days.  On an invoice, the cash discount terms are
usually followed by the net terms, which is the time in days allowed for ordinary payment of the
bill.  Thus, 3/10, Net 30 means that full payment is expected in thirty days if the cash discount of
3% is not taken for having paid the bill within ten days.  When the expression Terms Net Cash is
listed on a bill, it means that no deduction for early payment is allowed.  A trade discount is
normally applied to list prices by a manufacturer to show the actual price to retailers so that they
may know their cost and determine markups that will allow them to operate competitively and at
a profit.  A trade discount is applied by the seller to the list price and is independent of a cash or
time discount.  Discounts may also be used by manufacturers to adjust prices charged to
retailers without changing list prices.  This is usually done by series discounting and is
expressed as a series of percentages.  To compute a series discount, such as 40%, 20%, 10%,
first apply the 40% discount to the list price, then apply the 20% discount to the remainder, and
finally apply the 10% discount to the second remainder.

10. According to the above passage, trade discounts are                               10.____
    A.  applied by the buyer              B.  independent of cash discounts
    C.  restricted to cash sales          D.  used to secure rapid payment of bills

11. According to the above passage, if the sales terms 5/10, Net 60 appear on a       11.____
    bill in the amount of $100 dated December 5, 2016 and the buyer submits his
    payment on December 15, 2016, his PROPER payment should be
    A.  $60                  B.  $90                  C.  $95                  D.  $100

12. According to the above passage, if a manufacturer gives a trade discount of 40%   12.____
    for an item with a list price of $250 and the terms are Net Cash, the price a retail
    merchant is required to pay for this item is
    A.  $250         B.  $210         C.  $150         D.  $100

13. According to the above passage, a series discount of 25%, 20%, 10% applied   13.____
    to a list price of $200 results in an ACTUAL price to the buyer of
    A.  $88          B.  $90          C.  $108         D.  $110

14. According to the above passage, if a manufacturer gives a trade discount of 50%   14.____
    and the terms are 6/10, Net 30, the cost to a retail merchant of an item with a list
    price of $500 and for which he takes the time discount is
    A.  $220         B.  $235         C.  $240         D.  $250

Questions 15-22.

DIRECTIONS:   Questions 15 through 22 each show in Column I the information written on five
cards (lettered j, k, l, m, n) which have to be filed.  You are to choose the option
(lettered A, B, C, or D) in Column II which BEST represents the proper order of
filing according to the information, rules, and sample question given below.

A file card record is kept of the work assignments for all the employees in a certain
bureau.  On each card is the employee's name, the date of work assignment, and the work
assignment code number.  The cards are to be filed according to the following rules:

FIRST:     File in alphabetical order according to employee's name.

SECOND:  When two or more cards have the same employee's name, file according to
           the assignment date, beginning with the earliest date.

THIRD:     When two or more cards have the same employee's name and the same date,
           file according to the work assignment number beginning with the lowest
           number.

Column II shows the cards arranged in four different orders.  Pick the option (A, B, C, or D)
in Column II which shows the correct arrangement of the cards according to th above filing
rules.

SAMPLE QUESTION

Column I
j.  Cluney 4/8/02 (486503)
k.  Roster 5/10/01 (246611)
l.  Altool 10/15/02 (711433)
m.  Cluney 12/18/02 (527610)
n.  Cluney 4/8/02 (486500)

Column II
A.  k, l, m, j, n
B.  k, n, j, l, m
C.  l, k, j, m, n
D.  l, n, j, m, k

The correct way to file the cards is:
- l.   Altool 10/15/02 (71143)
- n.   Cluney 4/8/02 (486500)
- j.   Cluney 4/8/02 (486503)
- m.   Cluney 12/18/02 (527610)
- k.   Roster 5/10/01 (246611)

The correct filing order is shown by the letters l, n, j, m, k.  The answer to the sample question is the letter D, which appears in front of the letters l, n, j, m, k in Column II.

<u>COLUMN I</u>                                   <u>COLUMN II</u>

15.  j.   Smith 3/19/03 (662118)        A.  j, m, l, n, k           15._____
     k.   Turner 4/16/99 (481349)       B.  j, l, n, m, k
     l.   Terman 3/20/02 (210229)       C.  k, n, m, l, j
     m.  Smyth 3/20/02 (481359)         D.  j, n, k, l, m
     n.   Terry 5/11/01 (672128)

16.  j.   Ross 5/29/02 (396118)         A.  l, m, k, n, j           16._____
     k.   Rosner 5/29/02 (439281)       B.  m, l, k, n, j
     l.   Rose 7/19/02 (723456)         C.  l, m, k, j, n
     m.  Rosen 5/29/03 (829692)         D.  m, l, j, n, k
     n.   Ross 5/29/02 (399118)

17.  j.   Sherd 10/12/99 (552368)       A.  n, m, k, j, l           17._____
     k.   Snyder 11/12/99 (539286)      B.  j, m, l, k, n
     l.   Shindler 10/13/98 (426798)    C.  m, k, n, j. l
     m.  Scherld 10/12/99 (552386)      D.  m, n, j, l, k
     n.   Schneider 11/12/99 (798213)

18.  j.   Carter 1/16/02 (489636)       A.  k, n, j, l, m           18._____
     k.   Carson 2/16/01 (392671)       B.  n, k, m, l, j
     l.   Carter 1/16/01 (486936)       C.  n, k, l, j, m
     m.  Carton 3/15/00 (489639)        D.  k, n, l, j, m
     n.   Carson 2/16/01 (392617)

19.  j.   Thomas 3/18/99 (763182)       A.  m, l, j, k, n           19._____
     k.   Tompkins 3/19/00 (928439)     B.  j, m, l, k, n
     l.   Thomson 3/21/00 (763812)      C.  j, l, n, m, k
     m.  Thompson 3/18/99 (924893)      D.  l, m, j, n, k
     n.   Tompson 3/19/99 (928793)

20.  j.   Breit 8/10/03 (345612)        A.  m, j, n, k, l           20._____
     k.   Briet 5/21/00 (837543)        B.  n, m, j, k, l
     l.   Bright 9/18/99 (931827)       C.  m, j, k, l, n
     m.  Breit 3/7/98 (553984)          D.  j, m, k, l, n
     n.   Brent 6/14/04 (682731)

| COLUMN I | COLUMN II | |
|---|---|---|
| 21. j. Roberts 10/19/02 (581932)<br>k. Rogers 8/9/00 (638763)<br>l. Rogerts 7/15/97 (105689)<br>m. Robin 3/8/92 (287915)<br>n. Rogers 4/2/04 (736921) | A. n, k, l, m, j<br>B. n, k, l, j, m<br>C. k, n, l, m, j<br>D. j, m, k, n, l | 21.____ |
| 22. j. Hebert 4/28/02 (719468)<br>k. Herbert 5/8/01 (938432)<br>l. Helbert 9/23/04 (832912)<br>m. Herbst 7/10/03 (648599)<br>n. Herbert 5/8/01 (487627) | A. n, k, j, m, l<br>B. j, l, n, k, m<br>C. l, j, k, n, m<br>D. l, j, n, k, m | 22.____ |

23. In order to pay its employees, the Convex Company obtained bills and coins    23.____
in the following denominations:

| Denomination | $20 | $10 | $5 | $1 | $.50 | $.25 | $.10 | $.05 | $.01 |
|---|---|---|---|---|---|---|---|---|---|
| Number | 317 | 122 | 38 | 73 | 69 | 47 | 39 | 25 | 36 |

What was the TOTAL amount of cash obtained?
   A. $7,874.76    B. $7,878.00    C. $7,889.25    D. $7,924.35

24. H. Partridge receives a weekly gross salary (before deductions) of $596.25.    24.____
Through weekly payroll deductions of $19.77, he is paying back a load he took
from his pension fund.
If other fixed weekly deductions amount to $184.14, how much pay would Mr.
Partridge take home over a period of 33 weeks?
   A. $11,446.92    B. $12,375.69    C. $12,947.22    D. $19,676.25

25. Mr. Robertson is a city employee enrolled in a city retirement system. He has    25.____
taken out a loan from the retirement fund and is paying it back at the rate of
$14.90 every two weeks.
In eighteen weeks, how much money will he have paid back on the loan?
   A. $268.20    B. $152.80    C. $124.10    D. $67.05

26. In 2015, the Iridor Book Company had the following expenses: rent, $6,500;    26.____
overhead, $52,585; inventory, $35,700; and miscellaneous, $1,275.
If all of these expenses went up 18% in 2016, what would they TOTAL in 2016?
   A. $17,290.80    B. $78,768.20    C. $96,060.00    D. $113,350.80

27. Ms. Ranier had a gross salary of $355.36, paid once every week.    27.____
If the deductions from each paycheck are $62.72, $25.13, $6.29, and $1,27, how
much money would Ms. Ranier take home in four weeks?
   A. $1,039.80    B. $1,421.44    C. $2,079.60    D. $2,842.88

28. Mr. Martin had a net income of $19,100 for the year.
If he spent 34% on rent and household expenses, 3% on house furnishings, 25% on clothes, and 36% on food, how much was left for savings and other expenses?
   A. $196.00     B. $382.00     C. $649.40     D. $1,960.00

28.____

29. Mr. Elsberg can pay back a loan of $1,800 from the city employees' retirement system if he pays back $36.69 every two weeks for two full years.
At the end of the two years, how much more than the original $1,800 he borrowed will Mr. Elsberg have paid back?
   A. $53.94     B. $107.88     C. $190.79     D. $214.76

29.____

30. Mrs. Nusbaum is a city employee, receiving a gross salary (salary before deductions) of $31,200. Every two weeks, the following deductions are taken out of her salary: Federal Income Tax, $243.96; FICA, $66.39; State Tax, $44.58; City Tax, $20.91; Health Insurance, $4.71.
If Mrs. Nusbaum's salary and deductions remained the same for a full calendar year, what would her NET salary (gross salary less deductions) be in that year?
   A. $9,894.30     B. $21,305.70     C. $28,118.25     D. $30,819.45

30.____

# KEY (CORRECT ANSWERS)

| | | | | | |
|---|---|---|---|---|---|
| 1. | C | 11. | C | 21. | D |
| 2. | A | 12. | C | 22. | B |
| 3. | D | 13. | C | 33. | A |
| 4. | C | 14. | B | 24. | C |
| 5. | D | 15. | A | 25. | C |
| 6. | A | 16. | C | 26. | D |
| 7. | A | 17. | D | 27. | A |
| 8. | B | 18. | C | 28. | B |
| 9. | B | 19. | B | 29. | B |
| 10. | B | 20. | A | 30. | B |

# EXAMINATION SECTION
# TEST 1

DIRECTIONS: Each question or incomplete statement is followed by several suggested answers or completions. Select the one that BEST answers the question or completes the statement. *PRINT THE LETTER OF THE CORRECT ANSWER IN THE SPACE AT THE RIGHT.*

Questions 1-5.

DIRECTIONS: Questions 1 through 5 are to be answered on the basis of the statement account shown below.

## STATEMENT OF ACCOUNT

Regal Tools, Inc.
136 Culver Street
Cranston, R.I. 02910

TO:   Vista, Inc.                              DATE:   March 31
      572 No. Copeland Ave.
      Pawtucket, R.I. 02800

| DATE | ITEM | CHARGES | PAYMENTS AND CREDITS | BALANCE |
|------|------|---------|----------------------|---------|
|  | Previous Balance |  |  | 785.35 |
| March   8 | Payment |  | 785.35 | ---- |
| 12 | Invoice 17-582 | 550 -- |  | 550.00 |
| 17 | Invoice 17-692 | 700 -- |  | 1250.00 |
| 31 | Payment |  | 550.00 | 700.00 |

PAY LAST AMOUNT SHOWN IN BALANCE COLUMN

1.  Which company is the customer?                                           1._____

2.  What total amount was charged by the customer during March?             2._____

3.  How much does the customer owe on March 31?                             3._____

4.  On which accounting schedule would Vista list Regal?                    4._____

5.  The terms on invoice 17-582 were 3/20, n/45.                            5._____
    What was the CORRECT amount for which the check should have been written when payment was made?

6. Which item is NOT a source document? A(n)

   6.__

   A. invoice
   C. punched card
   B. magnetic tape
   D. telephone conversation

7. What is double-entry accounting?

   7.__

   A. Journalizing and posting
   B. Recording debit and credit parts for a transaction
   C. Using carbon paper when preparing a source document
   D. Posting a debit or credit and computing the new account balance

8. The balance in the asset account Supplies is $600. An ending inventory shows $200 of supplies on hand.
   The adjusting entry should be

   8.__

   A. debit Supplies Expense for $200, credit Supplies for $200
   B. credit Supplies Expense for $200, debit Supplies for $200
   C. debit Supplies Expense for $400, credit Supplies for $400
   D. credit Supplies Expense for $400, debit Supplies for $400

9. What is the purpose of preparing an Income Statement? To

   9.__

   A. report the net income or net loss
   B. show the owner's claims against the assets
   C. prove that the accounting equation is in balance
   D. prove that the total debits equal the total credits

10. Which account does NOT belong on the Income Statement?

   10.__

   A. Salaries Payable
   B. Rental Revenue
   C. Advertising Expense
   D. Sales Returns and Allowances

11. The source document for entries made in a Purchases Journal is a purchase

   11.__

   A. order     B. requisition     C. invoice     D. register

12. A business check guaranteed for payment by the bank is called a

   12.__

   A. bank draft
   C. cashier's check
   B. certified check
   D. personal check

13. The entry that closes the Purchases Account contains a

   13.__

   A. debit to Purchases
   B. debit to Purchases Returns and Allowances
   C. credit to Purchases
   D. credit to Income and Expense Summary

14. Which account would NOT appear on a Balance Sheet?　　　　　　　　　　　　14.____

    A. Office Equipment　　　　　　　　B. Transportation In
    C. Mortgage Payable　　　　　　　　D. Supplies on Hand

15. Which entry is made at the end of the fiscal period for the purpose of updating the Pre-　　15.____
paid Insurance Account?
_____ entry.

    A. Correcting　　　　B. Closing　　　　C. Adjusting　　　　D. Reversing

16. Which deduction from gross pay is NOT required by law?　　　　　　　　　　16.____

    A. Hospitalization insurance
    B. FICA tax
    C. Federal income tax
    D. New York State income tax

17. What is the last date on which a 2 percent cash discount can be taken for an invoice　　17.____
dated October 15 with terms of 2/10, n/30?

    A. October 15　　　　　　　　B. October 17
    C. October 25　　　　　　　　D. November 14

18. Which item on the bank reconciliation statement would require the business to record a　18.____
journal entry?
A(n)

    A. deposit in transit　　　　　　B. outstanding check
    C. canceled check　　　　　　　D. bank service charge

19. Which is NOT an essential component of a computer?　　　　　　　　　　　19.____
A(n)

    A. input device　　　　　　　　B. central processor
    C. output device　　　　　　　　D. telecommunicator

20. Which group of accounts could appear on a post-closing trial balance?　　　　　20.____

    A. Petty Cash; Accounts Receivable; FICA Taxes Payable
    B. Office Furniture; Office Expense; Supplies on Hand
    C. Supplies Expense; Sales; Advertising Expense
    D. Sales Discount; Rent Expense; J. Smith, Drawing

21. The withdrawals of cash by the owner are recorded in the owner's drawing account as　21.____
a(n)

    A. adjusting entry　　　　　　　B. closing entry
    C. credit　　　　　　　　　　　D. debit

22. An account in the General Ledger which shows a total of a related Subsidiary Ledger is　22.____
referred to as a(n) _____ account.

    A. revenue　　　　　　　　　　B. controlling
    C. temporary　　　　　　　　　D. owner's equity

23.

For Deposit Only
Anthony Hill

Which type of endorsement is shown above?

A. Restrictive
C. Full
B. Blank
D. Qualified

23.____

24. Which is a chronological record of all the transactions of a business?

A. Worksheet
C. Journal
B. Income Statement
D. Trial balance

24.____

25. Which error would NOT be revealed by the preparation of a trial balance?

A. Posting of an entire transaction more than once
B. Incorrectly pencil footing the balance of a general ledger account
C. Posting a debit of $320 as $230
D. Omitting an account with a balance

25.____

26. The Cash Receipts Journal is used to record the

A. purchase of merchandise for cash
B. purchase of merchandise on credit
C. sale of merchandise for cash
D. sale of merchandise on credit

26.____

27. On a systems flowchart, which symbol is commonly used to indicate the direction of the flow of work?
A(n)

A. arrow
B. circle
C. diamond
D. rectangle

27.____

28. Which account balance would be eliminated by a closing entry at the end of the fiscal period?

A. Office Equipment
C. Owner's Capital
B. Owner's Drawing
D. Mortgage Payable

28.____

29. In a data processing system, the handling and manipulation of data according to precise procedures is called

A. input
C. storage
B. processing
D. output

29.____

30. Which financial statement reflects the cumulative financial position of the business?

A. Bank statement
C. Trial balance
B. Income statement
D. Balance sheet

30.____

31. Which account should be credited when recording a cash proof showing an overage?     31.____

    A. Sales
    B. Cash
    C. Cash Short and Over
    D. Sales Returns and Allowances

32. In which section of the income statement would the purchases account be shown?     32.____

    A. Cost of Goods Sold         B. Income from Sales
    C. Operating Expenses       D. Other Expenses

33. What is an invoice?     33.____
A(n)

    A. order for the shipment of goods
    B. order for the purchase of goods
    C. receipt for goods purchased
    D. statement listing goods purchased

34. A business uses a Sales Journal, a Purchases Journal, a Cash Receipts Journal, a Cash    34.____
Payments Journal, and a General Journal.
In which journal would a credit memorandum received from a creditor be recorded?
_____ Journal

    A. Sales             B. Purchases
    C. General          D. Cash Receipts

35. Which account is debited to record a weekly payroll?     35.____

    A. Employees Income Tax Payable
    B. FICA Taxes Payable
    C. General Expense
    D. Salaries Expense

# KEY (CORRECT ANSWERS)

| | | | |
|---|---|---|---|
| 1. | Vista, Inc. | 16. | A |
| 2. | $1,250 | 17. | C |
| 3. | $700 | 18. | D |
| 4. | Accts. Payable | 19. | D |
| 5. | $533.50 | 20. | A |
| 6. | D | 21. | D |
| 7. | B | 22. | B |
| 8. | C | 23. | A |
| 9. | A | 24. | C |
| 10. | A | 25. | A |
| 11. | C | 26. | C |
| 12. | B | 27. | A |
| 13. | C | 28. | B |
| 14. | D | 29. | B |
| 15. | C | 30. | D |

| | |
|---|---|
| 31. | C |
| 32. | A |
| 33. | D |
| 34. | C |
| 35. | D |

———————

# EXAMINATION SECTION
# TEST 1

DIRECTIONS: Each question or incomplete statement is followed by several suggested answers or completions. Select the one that BEST answers the question or completes the statement. *PRINT THE LETTER OF THE CORRECT ANSWER IN THE SPACE AT THE RIGHT.*

1. In the preparation of a balance sheet, failure to consider the inventory of office supplies will result in _____ assets and _____.    1.____

   A. overstating; overstating liabilities
   B. understating; overstating capital
   C. understating; understating capital
   D. overstating; understating liabilities

2. The annual federal unemployment tax is paid by the    2.____

   A. employer *only*
   B. employee *only*
   C. employer and the employee equally
   D. employee, up to a maximum of 30 cents per week, and the balance is paid by the employer

3. Which are NORMALLY considered as current assets?    3.____

   A. Bank overdrafts              B. Prepaid expenses
   C. Accrued expenses             D. Payroll taxes

4. What type of ledger account is a summary of a number of accounts in another ledger? The _____ account.    4.____

   A. controlling                  B. subsidiary
   C. asset                        D. proprietorship

5. The PRIMARY purpose of a petty cash fund is to    5.____

   A. provide a fund for paying all miscellaneous expenses
   B. take the place of the cash account
   C. provide a common drawing fund for the owners of the business
   D. avoid entering a number of small amounts in the Cash Payments Journal

6. In the absence of a written agreement, profits in a partnership would be divided    6.____

   A. in proportion to the investment of the partners
   B. on an equitable basis depending on the time and effort spent by the partners
   C. equally
   D. on a ratio of investment basis, giving the senior partner preference

7. Which account represents a subtraction or decrease to an income account?    7.____

   A. Purchase Returns & Allowances
   B. Sales Returns & Allowances
   C. Freight In
   D. Prepaid Rent

8. If the Interest Expense account showed a debit balance of $210 as of December 31, and $40 of this amount was prepaid on Notes Payable, which statement is CORRECT as of December 31?   8.____

   A. Prepaid Interest of $170 should be shown as a deferred expense in the balance sheet.
   B. Interest Expense should be shown in the Income Statement as $210.
   C. Prepaid Interest of $40 should be listed as a deferred credit to income in the balance sheet.
   D. Interest Expense should be shown in the Income Statement as $170.

9. When prices are rising, which inventory-valuation method results in the LOWEST inventory value?   9.____

   A. FIFO
   C. Average cost
   B. LIFO
   D. Declining balance

10. Which of the following is a CORRECT procedure in preparing a bank reconciliation?   10.____

   A. Deposits in transit should be added to the cash balance on the books, and outstanding checks should be deducted from the cash balance on the bank statement.
   B. The cash balance on the bank statement and the cash balance on the books should be equal if there are deposits in transit and outstanding checks.
   C. Outstanding checks should be deducted from the cash balance on the books.
   D. Any service charge should be deducted from the check stub balance.

11. Which ratio indicates that there may NOT be enough on hand to meet current obligations?   11.____

   A. $\frac{\text{fixed assets}}{\text{fixed liabilities}} = \frac{2}{3}$
   B. $\frac{\text{total assets}}{\text{total obligations}} = \frac{3}{5}$
   C. $\frac{\text{current assets}}{\text{current liabilities}} = \frac{1}{3}$
   D. $\frac{\text{current assets}}{\text{fixed liabilities}} = \frac{1}{2}$

12. Which asset is NOT subject to depreciation?   12.____

   A. Factory equipment
   C. Buildings
   B. Land
   D. Machinery

13. Which form is prepared to verify that the total of the account balances in the Customers Ledger agrees with the balance in the controlling account in the General Ledger?   13.____

   A. Worksheet
   B. Schedule of accounts payable
   C. Schedule of accounts receivable
   D. Trial balance

14. If the merchandise inventory on hand at the end of the year was overstated, what will be the result of this error?    14._____

    A. *Understatement* of income for the year
    B. *Overstatement* of income for the year
    C. *Understatement* of assets at the end of the year
    D. No effect on income or assets

15. Working capital is found by subtracting the total current liabilities from the total    15._____

    A. fixed liabilities    B. fixed assets
    C. current income    D. current assets

16. Which is the CORRECT procedure for calculating the rate of merchandise turnover?    16._____

    A. Gross Sales divided by Net Sales
    B. Cost of Sales divided by Average Inventory
    C. Net Purchases divided by Average Inventory
    D. Gross Purchases divided by Net Purchases

17. The books of the Atlas Cement Corporation show a net profit of $142,000. To close the Profit and Loss account of the corporation at the end of the year, the account CREDITED should be    17._____

    A. Earned Surplus    B. Capital Stock
    C. C. Atlas, Capital    D. C. Atlas, Personal

18. The bank statement at the end of the month indicated a bank charge for printing a new checkbook.
How is this information recorded?
Debit    18._____

    A. Cash and credit Office Supplies
    B. Office Supplies and credit the Bank Charges
    C. the Bank Charges and credit Office Supplies
    D. Miscellaneous Expense and credit Cash

19. The Allowance for Doubtful Accounts appears on the balance sheet as a deduction from    19._____

    A. Accounts Receivable    B. Notes Receivable
    C. Accounts Payable    D. Notes Payable

20. The Tucker Equipment Corporation had a $45,000 profit for the year ended December 31.
Which would be the PROPER entry to close the Income and Expense account at the end of the year?
Debit Income and Expense Summary; credit    20._____

    A. Tucker, Capital    B. Tucker, Drawing
    C. Retained Earnings    D. Capital Stock

21. A failure to record a purchases invoice would be discovered when the          21.____

    A. monthly statement of account is sent to the customer
    B. check is received from the customer
    C. check is sent to the creditor
    D. statement of account is received from the creditor

22. Which General Ledger account would appear in a post-closing trial balance?          22.____

    A. Notes Receivable          B. Bad Debts Expense
    C. Sales Discount            D. Fee Income

23. Which deduction is affected by the number of exemptions claimed?          23.____

    A. State Disability          B. State income tax
    C. FICA tax               D. Workers' Compensation

24. The face value of a 60-day, 12% promissory note is $900.          24.____
The maturity value of this note will be

    A. $909        B. $900        C. $918        D. $1,008

25. An invoice dated March 10, terms 2/10, n/30, should be paid no later than          25.____

    A. March 20        B. March 31        C. April 9        D. April 10

# KEY (CORRECT ANSWERS)

| | | | | |
|---|---|---|---|---|
| 1. | C | | 11. | C |
| 2. | A | | 12. | B |
| 3. | B | | 13. | C |
| 4. | A | | 14. | B |
| 5. | D | | 15. | D |
| 6. | C | | 16. | B |
| 7. | B | | 17. | A |
| 8. | D | | 18. | D |
| 9. | B | | 19. | A |
| 10. | D | | 20. | C |

| | |
|---|---|
| 21. | D |
| 22. | A |
| 23. | B |
| 24. | C |
| 25. | C |

# TEST 2

DIRECTIONS: Each question or incomplete statement is followed by several suggested answers or completions. Select the one that BEST answers the question or completes the statement. *PRINT THE LETTER OF THE CORRECT ANSWER IN THE SPACE AT THE RIGHT.*

1. Which is NOT an essential element of a computer system?    1.____

   A. Input                          B. Central processing unit
   C. Verifier                       D. Output

2. The general ledger account that would NOT appear in a post-closing trial balance would be    2.____

   A. Cash                           B. Accounts Payable
   C. Furniture and Fixtures         D. Sales Income

3. Ralph Hanley, age 45, supports his wife and three children.    3.____
   Mr. Hanley is the only member of the family required to file an income tax return.
   What is the MAXIMUM number of exemptions he can claim?

   A. One          B. Five          C. Three          D. Four

4. The cost of a fixed asset minus the allowance for depreciation (accumulated deprecia-tion) is the _____ value.    4.____

   A. market       B. cost          C. liquidation    D. book

5. The form used by a bookkeeper in summarizing adjustments and information which will be used in preparing statements is called a    5.____

   A. journal                        B. balance sheet
   C. ledger                         D. worksheet

6. When a large number of transactions of a particular kind are to be entered in bookkeep-ing records, it is USUALLY advisable to use    6.____

   A. cash records                   B. controlling accounts
   C. special journals               D. special ledgers

7. The petty cash book shows a petty cash balance of $9.80 on May 31. The petty cash box contains only $9.10.    7.____
   What account will be debited to record the $.70 difference?

   A. Cash                           B. Petty Cash
   C. Cash Short and Over            D. Petty Cash Expense

8. The ONLY difference between the books of a partnership and those of a sole proprietor-ship appears in the _____ accounts.    8.____

   A. proprietorship                 B. liability
   C. asset                          D. expense

9. The earnings of a corporation are FIRST recorded as a credit to an account called    9.____

   A. Dividends Payable              B. Capital Stock Authorized
   C. Retained Earnings              D. Profit and Loss Summary

10. A firm purchased a new delivery truck for $2,900 and sold it four years later for $500. The Allowance for Depreciation of Delivery Equipment account was credited for $580 at the end of each of the four years.
When the machine was sold, there was a

    A. loss of $80                  B. loss of $1,820
    C. loss of $2,400           D. gain of $80

10.\_\_\_\_

11. FICA taxes are paid by

    A. employees *only*
    B. employers *only*
    C. both employees and employers
    D. neither employees nor employers

11.\_\_\_\_

12. Which phase of the data processing cycle is the SAME as calculating net pay in a manual system?

    A. Input        B. Processing        C. Storing        D. Output

12.\_\_\_\_

13. Which error will cause the trial balance to be out of balance?

    A. A sales invoice for $60 was entered in the Sales Journal for $600.
    B. A credit to office furniture in the journal was posted as a credit to office machines in the ledger.
    C. A debit to advertising expense in the journal was posted as a debit to miscellaneous expense in the ledger.
    D. A debit to office equipment in the journal was posted as a credit to office equipment in the ledger.

13.\_\_\_\_

14. The collection of a bad debt previously written off will result in a(n)

    A. *decrease* in assets          B. *decrease* in capital
    C. *increase* in assets          D. *increase* in liabilities

14.\_\_\_\_

15. Which account does NOT belong in the group?

    A. Notes Receivable          B. Building
    C. Office Equipment         D. Delivery Truck

15.\_\_\_\_

16. The adjusting entry to record the estimated bad debts is debit _____ and credit _____.

    A. Allowance for Bad Debts; Bad Debts Expense
    B. Bad Debts Expense; Allowance for Bad Debts
    C. Allowance for Bad Debts; Accounts Receivable
    D. Bad Debts Expense; Accounts Receivable

16.\_\_\_\_

17. At the end of the year, which account should be closed into the income and expense summary?

    A. Freight In          B. Allowance for Doubtful Accounts
    C. Notes Receivable        D. Petty Cash

17.\_\_\_\_

18. Which form is prepared to aid in verifying that the customer's account balances in the customer's ledger agree with the balance in the Accounts Receivable account in the general ledger?

    A.  Worksheet
    B.  Schedule of Accounts Payable
    C.  Schedule of Accounts Receivable
    D.  Trial Balance

18.____

19. In the preparation of an income statement, failure to consider accrued wages will result in

    A.  *overstating* operating expense and understating net profit
    B.  *overstating* net profit *only*
    C.  *understating* operating expense and overstating net profit
    D.  *understating* operating expense *only*

19.____

20. The CORRECT formula for determining the rate of merchandise turnover is

    A.  cost of goods sold divided by average inventory
    B.  net sales divided by net purchases
    C.  gross sales divided by ending inventory
    D.  average inventory divided by cost of goods sold

20.____

21. A legal characteristic of a corporation is _____ liability.

    A.  contingent           B.  limited
    C.  unlimited           D.  deferred

21.____

22. A customer's check you had deposited is returned to you by the bank labeled *Dishonored.*
What entries would be made as a result of this action? Debit _____ and credit _____.

    A.  cash; customer's account
    B.  miscellaneous expense; cash
    C.  customer's account; capital
    D.  customer's account; cash

22.____

23. The TOTAL capital of a corporation may be found by adding

    A.  assets and liabilities
    B.  assets and capital stock
    C.  liabilities and capital stock
    D.  earned surplus and capital stock

23.____

24. The source of an entry made in the Petty Cash book is the

    A.  general ledger          B.  voucher
    C.  register            D.  general journal

24.____

25. Which account is debited to record interest earned but not yet due?

    A.  Deferred Interest
    B.  Interest Receivable
    C.  Interest Income
    D.  Income and Expense Summary

25.____

# KEY (CORRECT ANSWERS)

| | | | | |
|---|---|---|---|---|
| 1. | C | | 11. | C |
| 2. | D | | 12. | B |
| 3. | B | | 13. | D |
| 4. | D | | 14. | C |
| 5. | D | | 15. | A |
| 6. | C | | 16. | B |
| 7. | C | | 17. | A |
| 8. | A | | 18. | C |
| 9. | C | | 19. | C |
| 10. | A | | 20. | A |

21. B
22. D
23. D
24. B
25. B

# TEST 3

DIRECTIONS: Each question or incomplete statement is followed by several suggested answers or completions. Select the one that BEST answers the question or completes the statement. *PRINT THE LETTER OF THE CORRECT ANSWER IN THE SPACE AT THE RIGHT.*

1. Which reason should NOT generally be used by an employer when making a hiring decision?
   An applicant('s)

   A. resume reveals a lack of job-related skills
   B. attendance record on a previous job is poor
   C. has improperly prepared the job application
   D. is married

   1.____

2. Graves, Owens, and Smith formed a partnership and invested $15,000 each. If the firm made a profit of $18,000 last year and profits and losses were shared equally, what was Owens' share of the net profit?

   A. $1,000    B. $5,000    C. $6,000    D. $9,000

   2.____

3. The bank statement balance of the Bedford Co. on May 31 was $3,263.28. The checkbook balance was $3,119.06. A reconciliation showed that the outstanding checks totaled $147.22 and that there was a bank service charge of $3.00. The CORRECT checkbook balance should be

   A. $3,260.28    B. $3,122.06    C. $3,116.06    D. $3,266.28

   3.____

4. Which account is shown in a post-closing trial balance?

   A. Prepaid Insurance    B. Fees Income
   C. Purchases            D. Freight In

   4.____

5. A check endorsed *For deposit only (signed) Samuel Jones* is an example of a _____ endorsement.

   A. full    B. blank    C. complete    D. restrictive

   5.____

6. The selling price of a share of stock as published in a daily newspaper is called the _____ value.

   A. book    B. face    C. par    D. market

   6.____

7. Which is obtained by dividing the cost of goods sold by the average inventory?

   A. Current ratio
   B. Merchandise inventory turnover
   C. Average rate of mark-up
   D. Acid-test ratio

   7.____

8. A Suzuki truck costing $39,000 is expected to have a useful life of six years and a salvage value of $3,000.
   If $6,000 is debited to the depreciation expense account each year for six years, what method of depreciation is used?

   A. Units of production    B. Straight line
   C. Declining balance      D. Sum of the years digits

   8.____

31

9. Which form is prepared to aid in verifying that the customer's account balances in the customer's ledger agree with the balance in the Accounts Receivable account in the General Ledger?

    A. Worksheet
    B. Schedule of Accounts Payable
    C. Schedule of Accounts Receivable
    D. Trial Balance

9.____

10. In the preparation of a balance sheet, failure to consider commissions owed to salespersons will result in _____ liabilities and _____ capital.

    A. understating; overstating
    B. understating; understating
    C. overstating; overstating
    D. overstating; understating

10.____

11. A financial statement generated by a computer is an example of a(n)

    A. audit trail
    C. input
    B. output
    D. program

11.____

12. Merchandise was sold for $150 cash plus a 3% sales tax.
The CORRECT credit(s) should be

    A. Sales Income $150, Sales Taxes Payable $4.50
    B. Sales Income $154.50
    C. Merchandise $150, Sales Taxes Payable $4.50
    D. Sales Income $150

12.____

13. The bookkeeper should prepare a bank reconciliation MAINLY to determine

    A. which checks are outstanding
    B. whether the checkbook balance and the bank statement balance are in agreement
    C. the total amount of checks written during the month
    D. the total amount of cash deposited during the month

13.____

14. Which is the CORRECT procedure for calculating the rate of merchandise turnover?

    A. Gross Sales divided by Net Sales
    B. Cost of Goods Sold divided by Average Inventory
    C. Net Purchases divided by Average Inventory
    D. Gross Purchases divided by Net Purchases

14.____

15. Which previous job should be listed FIRST on a job application form?
The

    A. least recent job
    C. job you liked best
    B. most recent job
    D. job which paid the most

15.____

16. Failure to record cash sales will result in

    A. *overstatement* of profit
    B. *understatement* of profit
    C. *understatement* of liabilities
    D. *overstatement* of capital

16.____

17. When a fixed asset is repaired, the cost of the repairs should be _____ account.    17._____

    A.  *debited* to the asset
    B.  *debited* to the expense
    C.  *credited* to the proprietor's capital
    D.  *credited* to the asset

18. The form used by a bookkeeper to summarize information which will be used in preparing financial statements is called a    18._____

    A.  journal
    C.  ledger
    B.  balance sheet
    D.  worksheet

19. Which type of ledger account is a summary of a number of accounts in another ledger?    19._____
_____ account.

    A.  Controlling
    C.  Asset
    B.  Subsidiary
    D.  Proprietorship

20. What is the summary entry on the Purchases Journal?    20._____
Debit _____ and credit _____.

    A.  Accounts Payable; Merchandise Purchases
    B.  Accounts Receivable; Merchandise Purchases
    C.  Merchandise Purchases; Accounts Receivable
    D.  Merchandise Purchases; Accounts Payable

21. The source document for entries made in the Sales Journal is a(n)    21._____

    A.  credit memo
    C.  invoice
    B.  statement of accounts
    D.  bill of lading

22. A Trial Balance which is in balance would NOT reveal the    22._____

    A.  omission of the credit part of an entry
    B.  posting of the same debit twice
    C.  omission of an entire transaction
    D.  omission of an account with a balance

23. A financial statement prepared by a computerized accounting system is an example of    23._____

    A.  input
    C.  flowcharting
    B.  output
    D.  programming

24. The form which the payroll clerk gives to each employee to show gross earnings and taxes withheld for the year is a    24._____

    A.  W-2      B.  W-3      C.  W-4      D.  1040

25. Who would be the LEAST appropriate reference on an application for a job?    25._____
A

    A.  relative
    B.  guidance counselor
    C.  former employer
    D.  prominent member of the community

---

# KEY (CORRECT ANSWERS)

| | | | | |
|---|---|---|---|---|
| 1. | D | | 11. | B |
| 2. | C | | 12. | A |
| 3. | C | | 13. | B |
| 4. | A | | 14. | B |
| 5. | D | | 15. | B |
| | | | | |
| 6. | D | | 16. | B |
| 7. | B | | 17. | B |
| 8. | B | | 18. | D |
| 9. | C | | 19. | A |
| 10. | A | | 20. | D |

| | |
|---|---|
| 21. | C |
| 22. | C |
| 23. | B |
| 24. | A |
| 25. | A |

---

# EXAMINATION SECTION
## TEST 1

DIRECTIONS:   Each question or incomplete statement is followed by several suggested
answers or completions. Select the one that BEST answers the question or
completes the statement. *PRINT THE LETTER OF THE CORRECT ANSWER
IN THE SPACE AT THE RIGHT.*

1.  On the 2016 profit and loss statement of a firm, *Salaries* was listed as $15,250. The bal-      1.____
ance sheet on December 31, 2015 showed accrued salaries of $525; the balance sheet
on December 31, 2016 showed prepaid salaries of $240 and accrued salaries of $600.
During 2016, cash paid for salaries amounted to

    A.  $15,250        B.  $15,085        C.  $14,890        D.  $15,415

2.  B began business March 15 with a cash investment of $25,000. The records show:      2.____
    Sales for the balance of the year                     $56,000
    Accounts Receivable, 12/31                  30,000
    Accounts Payable, 12/31                    20,000
    Inventory, 12/31                           24,000
    Gross profit mark-up on selling price, 25%
    The TOTAL cost of merchandise purchased during the year was

    A.  $42,000        B.  $66,000        C.  $20,000        D.  $44,000

3.  In the problem above, the cash balance on December 31 was      3.____

    A.  $81,000        B.  $51,000        C.  $5,000        D.  $9,000

4.  After Mr. S had been in business for a year, he ascertained the following facts:      4.____
    Sales                                        $80,000
    Raw materials used during the year at cost     30,000
    Labor                                   50,000
    Overhead                              8,000
    Work-in-process inventory, 12/31, at cost      18,000
    Finished goods inventory, 12/31, at selling price  25,000
    Assume that the mark-up has remained constant.
    The cost of manufacturing goods during the year was

    A.  $70,000                 B.  $88,000
    C.  $63,000                D.  none of the above

5.  In the problem above, the selling price of the goods manufactured during the year was      5.____

    A.  $50,000        B.  $55,000        C.  $80,000        D.  $105,000

6.  The furniture and fixtures account of a firm showed a balance on December 31, 2016 of      6.____
$9,500; the reserve for depreciation, furniture, and fixtures showed a balance of $6,540.
Depreciation has been taken at 10% per annum, straight-line method. On April 1, 2016,
a new machine was purchased for $500, for which an old machine, originally purchased
for $300 on October 1, 2013, was traded in with an allowance of $50, and the balance of
$450 was paid in cash. After making adjusting entries for 2016, the balance in the
reserve account should be

    A.  $7,505        B.  $6,465        C.  $7,430        D.  $7,415

7. Graves, Owens, and Smith formed a partnership and invested $15,000 each. If the firm made a profit of $18,000 last year and profits and losses were shared equally, what was Owens' share of the net profit?

    A. $1,000      B. $5,000      C. $6,000      D. $9,000

7.____

8. Brooks and Carton are partners with an investment of $50,000 and $25,000, respectively.
How much should be credited to Brooks as his share of a $60,000 profit if their agreement provides that the partners are to share profits and losses in proportion to their investments?

    A. $20,000      B. $30,000      C. $40,000      D. $50,000

8.____

9. The net worth of a corporation consisted of:
Preferred stock - 6% cumulative participating par value $100 per
    share, 2000 shares outstanding                   $200,000
Common stock - $50 par value, 3000 shares outstanding     150,000
Retained earnings                                  70,000
Common stockholders receive $3 a share after preferred stockholders receive 6% dividends; any remaining dividends are shared; $2 a share preferred, $1 a share common. Dividends have not yet been paid for the year.
The book value of a share of common stock is

    A. $63.33      B. $73.33      C. $50      D. $60

9.____

10. Mr. D, the owner of a small coat concern, has had a bookkeeper keep the records of the firm, but has not employed an accountant. He hires you to correct the work of the bookkeeper. The schedule of accounts payable on December 31 is as follows:
Ames                         $ 49
Bates                       740
Cohen (debit balance)      18
Other creditors         5000
You discover the following:
    I. Mr. D has paid Mr. C $175 on the basis of his personal memory of the purchase. The bill for $175 had been entered incorrectly in the Purchase Journal as $157.
    II. A refund of $35 from B, the result of an overpayment, had been entered in the Accounts Receivable column of the Cash Receipts Journal and had been posted to B's account.
    III. Mr. D bought $300 worth of goods from A on September 5. The entry had been recorded in the Purchase Journal and posted. On October 8, A bought a $50 coat from Mr. D. The entry was recorded in the Sales Journal and posted to the customer's ledger. On October 11, Mr. D sent a check to A to settle with him. He allowed a 2% discount on the sale and, therefore, sent a check for $251. This was entered in the Accounts Payable column of the Cash Payments Journal. No other entry was made.
The balance you found in the Accounts Payable account, before adjustments, was

    A. $5,740      B. $5,771      C. $5,701      D. $5,736

10.____

11. In the problem above, the balance in the Accounts Payable account after adjustments should be

    A. $5,670      B. $5,740      C. $5,789      D. $5,838

11.____

12. The balance of the Cash account in a firm's ledger on November 30 was $14,345     12._____
BEFORE consideration of the facts shown below.
The following facts were disclosed:
   I.   A $350 check was returned marked *Insufficient Funds*
  II.   Collections made at the end of November, but not yet deposited, $2,125
 III.   A bank debit memo for service charges, $5, was included with the bank statement
 IV.   A check written for $75 was entered in the checkbook as $57
  V.   Outstanding checks were:

| | |
|---|---|
| #439 | $ 76.00 |
| #441 | 85.00 |
| #442 (certified) | 100.00 |
| TOTAL | $261.00 |

The bank statement on November 30 should show a balance of

  A.   $12,708      B.   $12,044      C.   $12,008      D.   $12,108

---

# KEY (CORRECT ANSWERS)

| | | | |
|---|---|---|---|
| 1. | D | 7. | C |
| 2. | B | 8. | C |
| 3. | C | 9. | D |
| 4. | A | 10. | D |
| 5. | D | 11. | B |
| 6. | C | 12. | C |

---

# TEST 2

1. The valuation account classified in the current assets section of the balance sheet is                 1.____

   A. Allowance for Depreciation
   B. Reserve for Contingencies
   C. Allowance for Bad Debts
   D. Reserve for Discounts

2. The source for entries in the purchases journal is the purchase                 2.____

   A. order                    B. requisition
   C. invoice                  D. memo

3. Insurance premiums paid on the lives of salaried officers of corporations, where the cor-                 3.____
   poration is the beneficiary in case of death, are deductible expenses of the corporation
   PROVIDED that

   A. an appropriate increase in surrender value is shown as a credit to surplus
   B. life insurance premiums are not shown as expenses on corporate books
   C. life insurance premiums are charged to the *salaries* account of the officers
   D. a *loans payable* account is to be set up on the books

4. A transaction which will cause an increase in the net worth of a business is                 4.____

   A. purchase of $1,000 merchandise for cash
   B. accommodation sale of $1,000 merchandise to a dealer
   C. loan of $1,000 made by the proprietor
   D. sale of $1,000 merchandise to a customer

5. Working capital is found by                 5.____

   A. dividing current assets by current liabilities
   B. dividing current assets into current liabilities
   C. subtracting current liabilities from current assets
   D. subtracting current assets from current liabilities

6. The financial statement prepared for an estate, showing the sources from which the total                 6.____
   cash to be distributed was obtained, is called a Statement of

   A. Variation of Net Profit
   B. Application of Funds
   C. Affairs
   D. Realization and Liquidation

7. The depreciated value of an asset based on replacement or appraised value is known as                 7.____
   _____ value.

   A. book          B. assessed          C. net          D. sound

8. The inventory method resulting in balance sheet figures which are CLOSEST to present    8._____
cost is

   A. FIFO       B. LIFO       C. c/mkt       D. physical

9. Current assets $100,000; Fixed assets $50,000; Sales $200,000; Expenses $30,000;    9._____
Current liabilities $40,000. The working capital turnover is

   A. $60,000       B. 2.5:1       C. 3.33       D. 20:3

10. The premium on a $75,000 fire insurance policy from January 1, 2015 to January 1, 2018    10._____
is $900. On December 30, 2015, there was a fire loss of $50,000, which was subse-
quently paid by the insurance company.
The balance sheet value of the prepaid insurance on December 31, 2016 is

   A. $100       B. $150       C. $200       D. $400

11. F purchased an annuity policy at a total cost of $18,000. Starting on January 1, he began    11._____
to receive an annual payment of $1,500. His life expectancy as of that date was 16 years.
The amount of annuity income to be included in his gross income for the year on his
Federal income tax return is

   A. $375       B. $540       C. $1125       D. $1500

12. The costs and expenses for the G Sales Co. for the year ended December 31 were:    12._____
    Fixed               $100,000
    Variable          $375,000
The variable expenses were 75% of net sales.
The *break-even point* is

   A. $500,000       B. $400,000       C. $475,000       D. $550,000

---

# KEY (CORRECT ANSWERS)

| 1. | C | | 7. | D |
|----|---|---|----|---|
| 2. | C | | 8. | B |
| 3. | A | | 9. | C |
| 4. | D | | 10. | A |
| 5. | C | | 11. | A |
| 6. | D | | 12. | B |

---

# INTERPRETING STATISTICAL DATA
# GRAPHS, CHARTS AND TABLES
## EXAMINATION SECTION
## TEST 1

DIRECTIONS:  Each question or incomplete statement is followed by several suggested answers or completions. Select the one that BEST answers the question or completes the statement. *PRINT THE LETTER OF THE CORRECT ANSWER IN THE SPACE AT THE RIGHT.*

Questions 1-8.

DIRECTIONS:  Questions 1 through 8 are to be answered SOLELY on the basis of the information and chart given below.

    The following chart shows expenses in five selected categories for a one-year period expressed as percentages of these same expenses during the previous year. The chart compares two different offices. In Office T (represented by [      ] ) a cost reduction program has been tested for the past year. The other office, Office Q (represented by /////// ) served as a control, in that no special effort was made to reduce costs during the past year.

### RESULTS OF OFFICE COST REDUCTION PROGRAM

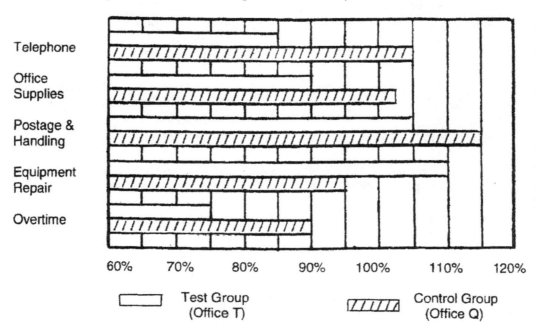

Expenses of Test and Control Groups for 2019
Expressed as Percentages of Same Expenses for 2018

1. In Office T, which category of expenses showed the GREATEST percentage reduction from 2018 to 2019?
   A. Telephone
   B. Office Supplies
   C. Postage and Mailing
   D. Overtime
   1._____

2. In which expense category did Office T show the BEST results in percentage terms when compared to Office Q?
   A. Telephone
   B. Office Supplies
   C. Postage and Mailing
   D. Overtime
   2._____

3. According to the above chart, the cost reduction program was LEAST effective for the expense category of
   A. Office Supplies
   B. Postage and Mailing
   C. Equipment Repair
   D. Overtime
   3._____

4. Office T's telephone costs went down during 2019 by APPROXIMATELY how many percentage points?
   A. 15
   B. 20
   C. 85
   D. 105
   4._____

5. Which of the following changes occurred in expenses for Office Supplies in Office Q in the year 2019 as compared with the year 2018?
   They
   A. *increased* by more than 100%
   B. *remained* the same
   C. *decreased* by a few percentage points
   D. *increased* by a few percentage points
   5._____

6. For which of the following expense categories do the results in Office T and the results in Office Q differ MOST NEARLY by 10 percentage points?
   A. Telephone
   B. Postage and Mailing
   C. Equipment Repair
   D. Overtime
   6._____

7. In which expense category did Office Q's costs show the GREATEST percentage increase in 2019?
   A. Telephone
   B. Office Supplies
   C. Postage and Mailing
   D. Equipment Repair
   7._____

8. In Office T, by APPROXIMATELY what percentage did overtime expense change during the past year?
   It
   A. *increased* by 15%
   B. *increased* by 75%
   C. *decreased* by 10%
   D. *decreased* by 25%
   8._____

# KEY (CORRECT ANSWERS)

| | | | |
|---|---|---|---|
| 1. | D | 5. | D |
| 2. | A | 6. | B |
| 3. | C | 7. | C |
| 4. | A | 8. | D |

———————

# TEST 2

DIRECTIONS: Each question or incomplete statement is followed by several suggested answers or completions. Select the one that BEST answers the question or completes the statement. *PRINT THE LETTER OF THE CORRECT ANSWER IN THE SPACE AT THE RIGHT.*

Questions 1-7.

DIRECTIONS: Questions 1 through 7 are to be answered SOLELY on the basis of the information contained in the following graph which relates to the work of a public agency.

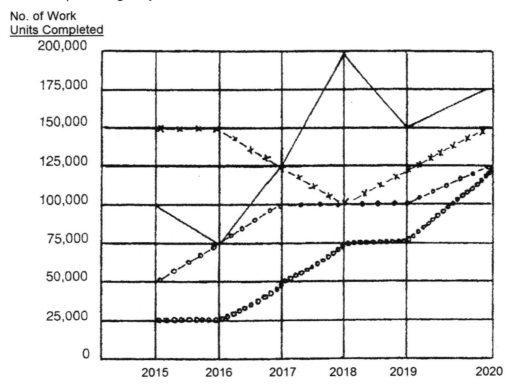

Units of each type of work completed by a public agency from 2015 to 2020.

Letters Written ———————————  Applications Processed -0-0-0-0-0
Documents Filed –x-x-x-x-x-x-x  Inspections Made 0000000000000

1. The year for which the number of units of one type of work completed was less than it was for the previous year while the number of each of the other types of work completed was more than it was for the previous year was
   A. 2016      B. 2017      C. 2018      D. 2019                                      1.____

2. The number of letters written exceeded the number of applications processed by the same amount in _____ of the years.
   A. two       B. three     C. four      D. five                                      2.____

3. The year in which the number of each type of work completed was GREATER 3.____
   than in the preceding year was
   A. 2017        B. 2018        C. 2019        D. 2020

4. The number of applications processed and the number of documents filed 4.____
   were the SAME in
   A. 2016        B. 2017        C. 2018        D. 2019

5. The TOTAL number of units of work completed by the agency 5.____
   A. increased in each year after 2015
   B. decreased from the prior year in two of the years after 2015
   C. was the same in two successive years from 2015 to 2020
   D. was less in 2015 than in any of the following years

6. For the year in which the number of letters written was twice as high as it was 6.____
   in 2015, the number of documents filed was _____ it was in 2015.
   A. the same as                    B. two-thirds of what
   C. five-sixths of what            D. one and one-half times what

7. The variable which was the MOST stable during the period 2015 through 2020 7.____
   was
   A. Inspections Made               B. Letters Written
   C. Documents Filed                D. Applications Processed

# KEY (CORRECT ANSWERS)

| 1. | B | 5. | C |
|----|---|----|---|
| 2. | B | 6. | B |
| 3. | D | 7. | D |
| 4. | C |   |   |

# TEST 3

DIRECTIONS: Each question or incomplete statement is followed by several suggested answers or completions. Select the one that BEST answers the question or completes the statement. *PRINT THE LETTER OF THE CORRECT ANSWER IN THE SPACE AT THE RIGHT.*

Questions 1-10.

DIRECTIONS: Questions 1 through 10 are to be answered SOLELY on the basis of the REPORT OF TELEPHONE CALLS table given below.

| Dept. | No. of Stations | No. of Employees | No. of Incoming Calls In | | No. of Long Distance Calls in | | No. of Divisions |
|---|---|---|---|---|---|---|---|
| | | | 2019 | 2020 | 2019 | 2020 | |
| I | 11 | 40 | 3421 | 4292 | 72 | 54 | 5 |
| II | 36 | 330 | 10392 | 10191 | 75 | 78 | 18 |
| III | 53 | 250 | 85243 | 85084 | 103 | 98 | 8 |
| IV | 24 | 60 | 9675 | 10123 | 82 | 85 | 6 |
| V | 13 | 30 | 5208 | 5492 | 54 | 48 | 6 |
| VI | 25 | 35 | 7472 | 8109 | 86 | 90 | 5 |
| VII | 37 | 195 | 11412 | 11299 | 68 | 72 | 11 |
| VIII | 36 | 54 | 8467 | 8674 | 59 | 68 | 4 |
| IX | 163 | 306 | 294321 | 289968 | 289 | 321 | 13 |
| X | 40 | 83 | 9588 | 8266 | 93 | 89 | 5 |
| XI | 24 | 68 | 7867 | 7433 | 86 | 87 | 13 |
| XII | 50 | 248 | 10039 | 10208 | 101 | 95 | 30 |
| XIII | 10 | 230 | 7550 | 6941 | 28 | 21 | 10 |
| XVI | 25 | 103 | 14281 | 14392 | 48 | 40 | 5 |
| XV | 19 | 230 | 8475 | 206 | 38 | 43 | 8 |
| XVI | 22 | 45 | 4684 | 5584 | 39 | 48 | 10 |
| XVII | 41 | 58 | 10102 | 9677 | 49 | 52 | 6 |
| XVIII | 82 | 106 | 106242 | 105889 | 128 | 132 | 10 |
| XIX | 6 | 13 | 2649 | 2498 | 35 | 29 | 2 |
| XX | 16 | 30 | 1395 | 1468 | 78 | 90 | 2 |

TABLE – REPORT OF TELEPHONE CALLS

1. The department which had more than 106,000 incoming calls in 2019 but fewer than 250,000 is
   A. II      B. IX      C. XVIII      D. III        1._____

2. The department which has fewer than 8 divisions and more than 100 but fewer than 300 employees is
   A. VII      B. XIV      C. XV      D. XVIII        2._____

3. The department which had an increase in 2020 over 2019 in the number of both incoming and long distance calls but had an increase in long distance calls of not more than 3 was
   A. IV      B. VI      C. XVII      D. XVIII        3._____

4. The department which had a decrease in the number of incoming calls in 2020        4.____
   as compared to 2019 and has not less than 6 nor more than 7 divisions is
   A. IV                 B. V                 C. XVII               D. III

5. The department which has more than 7 divisions and more than 200                    5.____
   employees but fewer than 19 stations is
   A. XV                 B. III               C. XX                 D. XIII

6. The department having more than 10 divisions and fewer than 36 stations,            6.____
   which had an increase in long distance calls in 2020 over 2019, is
   A. XI                 B. VII               C. XVI                D. XVIII

7. The department which in 2020 had at least 7,250 incoming calls and a                7.____
   decrease in long distance calls from 2019 and has more than 50 stations is
   A. IX                 B. XII               C. XVIII              D. III

8. The department which has fewer than 25 stations, fewer than 100 employees,          8.____
   10 or more divisions, and showed an increase of at least 9 long distance calls
   in 2020 over 2019 is
   A. IX                 B. XVI               C. XX                 D. XIII

9. The department which has more than 50 but fewer than 125 employees and              9.____
   had more than 5,000 incoming calls in 2019 but not more than 10,000, and
   more than 60 long distance calls in 2020 but not more than 85, and has more
   than 24 stations is
   A. VIII               B. XIV               C. IV                 D. XI

10. If the number of departments showing an increase in long distance calls in         10.____
    2020 over 1999 exceeds the number showing a decrease in long distance calls
    in the same period, select the Roman numeral indicating the department
    having less than one station for each 10 employees, provided not more than 8
    divisions are served by that department.
    If the number of departments showing an increase in long distance calls in
    2020 over 2019 does not exceed the number showing a decrease in long
    distance calls in the same period, select the Roman numeral indicating the
    department having the SMALLEST number of incoming calls in 2020.
    A. III                B. XIII              C. XV                 D. XX

_____

# KEY (CORRECT ANSWERS)

| | | | |
|---|---|---|---|
| 1. | C | 6. | A |
| 2. | B | 7. | D |
| 3. | A | 8. | B |
| 4. | C | 9. | A |
| 5. | D | 10. | C |

---

# TEST 4

DIRECTIONS: Each question or incomplete statement is followed by several suggested answers or completions. Select the one that BEST answers the question or completes the statement. *PRINT THE LETTER OF THE CORRECT ANSWER IN THE SPACE AT THE RIGHT.*

Questions 1-6.

DIRECTIONS: Questions 1 through 6 are to be answered SOLELY on the basis of the information given in the following chart. This chart shows the results of a study made of the tasks performed by a stenographer during one day. Included in the chart are the time at which she started a certain task and, under the particular heading, the amount of time, in minutes, she took to complete the task, and explanations of telephone calls and miscellaneous activities. NOTE: The time spent at lunch should not be included in any of your calculations.

| PAMELA JOB STUDY | | | | | | | |
|---|---|---|---|---|---|---|---|
| NAME: Pamela Donald | | | | | | DATE: 9/26 | |
| JOB TITLE: Stenographer | | | | | | | |
| DIVISION: Stenographic Pool | | | | | | | |
| | | | | | | | |
| Time of Start of Task | TASKS PERFORMED | | | | | | Explanations of Telephone Calls and Miscellaneous Activities |
| | Taking Dictation | Typing | Filing | Telephone Work | Handling Mail | Misc. Activities | |
| 9:00 | | | | | 22 | | |
| 9:22 | | | | | | 13 | Picking up supplies |
| 9:35 | | | | | | 15 | Cleaning typewriter |
| 9:50 | 11 | | | | | | |
| 10:01 | | 30 | | | | | |
| 10:31 | | | | 8 | | | Call to Agency A |
| 10:39 | 12 | | | | | | |
| 10:51 | | | 10 | | | | |
| 11:01 | | | | 7 | | | Call from Agency B |
| 11:08 | | 30 | | | | | |
| 11:38 | 10 | | | | | | |
| 11:48 | | | | 12 | | | Call from Agency C |
| 12:00 | L U N C H | | | | | | |
| 1:00 | | | | | 28 | | |
| 1:28 | 13 | | | | | | |
| 1:41-2:13 | | 32 | | 12 | | | Call to Agency B |
| X | | | 15 | | | | |
| Y | | 50 | | | | | |
| 3:30 | 10 | | | | | | |
| 3:40 | | 21 | | | | | |
| 4:01 | | | | 9 | | | Call from Agency A |
| 4:10 | 35 | | | | | | |
| 4:45 | | 9 | | | | | |
| 4:54 | | | | | | 6 | Cleaning up desk |

SAMPLE QUESTION:
The total amount of time spent on miscellaneous activities in the morning is exactly equal to the total amount of time spent
  A. filing in the morning
  B. handling mail in the afternoon
  C. miscellaneous activities in the afternoon
  D. handling mail in the morning

Explanation of answer to sample question:
The total amount of time spent on miscellaneous activities in the morning equals 28 minutes (13 minutes for picking up supplies plus 15 minutes for cleaning the typewriter); and since it takes 28 minutes to handle mail in the afternoon, the answer is B.

1. The time labeled Y at which the stenographer started a typing assignment was
  A. 2:15          B. 2:25          C. 2:40          D. 2:50

1.____

2. The ratio of time spent on all incoming calls to time spent on all outgoing calls for the day was
  A. 5:7           B. 5:12          C. 7:5           D. 7:12

2.____

3. Of the following combinations of tasks, which ones take up exactly 80% of the total time spent on Tasks Performed during the day?
  A. Typing, Filing, Telephone Work, Handling Mail
  B. Taking Dictation, Filing, and Miscellaneous Activities
  C. Taking Dictation, Typing, Handling Mail, and Miscellaneous Activities
  D. Taking Dictation, Typing, Filing, and Telephone Work

3.____

4. The total amount of time spent transcribing or typing work is how much MORE than the total amount of time spent in taking dictation?
  A. 55 minutes                    B. 1 hour
  C. 1 hour 10 minutes             D. 1 hour 25 minutes

4.____

5. The GREATEST number of shifts in activities occurred between the times of
  A. 9:00 A.M. and 10:31 A.M.      B. 9:35 A.M. and 11:01 A.M.
  C. 10:31 A.M. and 12:00 Noon     D. 3:30 P.M. and 5:00 P.M.

5.____

6. The total amount of time spent on Taking Dictation in the morning plus the total amount of time spent on Filing in the afternoon is exactly EQUAL to the total amount of time spent on
  A. Typing in the afternoon minus the total amount of time spent on Telephone Work in the afternoon
  B. Typing in the morning plus the total amount of time spent on Miscellaneous Activities
  C. Dictation in the afternoon plus the total amount of time spent on Filing in the morning
  D. Typing in the afternoon minus the total amount of time spent in Handling Mail in the morning

6.____

50

# KEY (CORRECT ANSWERS)

1.　C
2.　C
3.　D
4.　B
5.　C
6.　D

_____

# TEST 5

DIRECTIONS: Each question or incomplete statement is followed by several suggested answers or completions. Select the one that BEST answers the question or completes the statement. *PRINT THE LETTER OF THE CORRECT ANSWER IN THE SPACE AT THE RIGHT.*

Questions 1-8.

DIRECTIONS: Questions 1 through 8 are to be answered SOLELY on the basis of the information given in the following table.

| | Bronx | | Brooklyn | | Manhattan | | Queens | | Richmond | |
|---|---|---|---|---|---|---|---|---|---|---|
| | May | June | May | June | May | June | May | June | May | June |
| Number of Clerks in Office Assigned To Issue Applications for Licenses | 3 | 4 | 6 | 8 | 6 | 8 | 3 | 5 | 2 | 4 |
| Number of Licenses Issued | 950 | 1010 | 1620 | 1940 | 1705 | 2025 | 895 | 1250 | 685 | 975 |
| Amount Collected in License Fees | $42,400 | $52,100 | $77,600 | $94,500 | $83,700 | $98,800 | $39,300 | $65,500 | $30,600 | $48,200 |
| Number of Inspectors | 4 | 5 | 6 | 7 | 7 | 8 | 4 | 5 | 2 | 4 |
| Number of Inspections Made | 420 | 450 | 630 | 710 | 690 | 740 | 400 | 580 | 320 | 440 |
| Number of Violations Found As a Result of Inspections | 211 | 153 | 352 | 378 | 320 | 385 | 256 | 304 | 105 | 247 |

1. Of the following statements, the one which is NOT accurate on the basis of an inspection of the information contained in the table is that, for each office, the increase from May to June in the number of
   A. inspectors was accompanied by an increase in the number of inspections made
   B. licenses issued was accompanied by an increase in the amount collected in license fees
   C. inspections made was accompanied by an increase in the number of violations found
   D. licenses issued was accompanied by an increase in the number of clerks assigned to issue applications for licenses
   1.____

2. The TOTAL number of licenses issued by all five offices in the Division in May was
   A. 4,800     B. 5,855     C. 6,865     D. 7,200
   2.____

3. The total number of inspectors in all five borough offices in June exceeded the number in May by MOST NEARLY
   A. 21%     B. 26%     C. 55%     D. 70%
   3.____

52

4. In the month of June, the number of violations found per inspection made was the HIGHEST in
   A. Brooklyn     B. Manhattan     C. Queens     D. Richmond

4.____

5. In the month of May, the average number of inspections made by an inspector in the Bronx was the same as the average number of inspections made by an inspector in
   A. Brooklyn     B. Manhattan     C. Queens     D. Richmond

5.____

6. Assume that in June all of the inspectors in the Division spent 7 hours a day making inspections on each of the 21 working days in the month.
   Then the average amount of time that an inspector in the Manhattan office spent on an inspection that month was MOST NEARLY
   A. 2 hours                   B. 1 hour and 35 minutes
   C. 1 hour and 3 minutes    D. 38 minutes

6.____

7. If an average fine of $100 was imposed for a violation found by the Division, what was the TOTAL amount in fines imposed for all the violations found by the Division in May?
   A. $124,400     B. $133,500     C. $146,700     D. $267,000

7.____

8. Assume that the amount collected in license fees by the entire Division in May was 80 percent of the amount collected by the entire Division in April.
   How much was collected by the entire Division in April?
   A. $218,880     B. $328,320     C. $342,000     D. $410,400

8.____

---

# KEY (CORRECT ANSWERS)

| 1. | C | 5. | A |
|----|---|----|---|
| 2. | B | 6. | B |
| 3. | B | 7. | A |
| 4. | D | 8. | C |

---

# TEST 6

DIRECTIONS: Each question or incomplete statement is followed by several suggested answers or completions. Select the one that BEST answers the question or completes the statement. *PRINT THE LETTER OF THE CORRECT ANSWER IN THE SPACE AT THE RIGHT.*

Questions 1-8.

DIRECTIONS: Questions 1 through 8 are to be answered SOLELY on the basis of the information contained in the chart and table shown below, which relate to Bureau X in a certain public agency. The chart shows the percentage of the bureau's annual expenditures spent on equipment, supplies, and salaries for each of the years 2016-2020. The table shows the bureau's annual expenditures for each of the years 2016-2020.

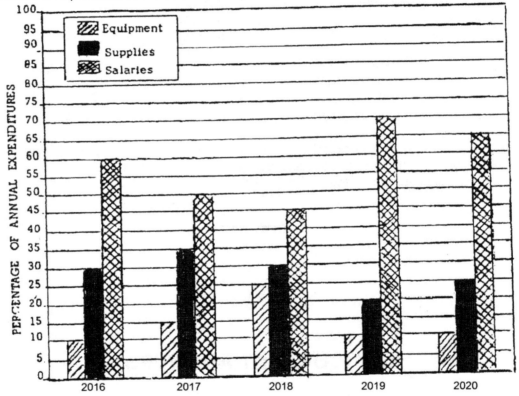

The bureau's annual expenditures for the years 2016-2020 are shown in the following table:

| YEAR | EXPENDITURES |
|------|-------------|
| 2016 | $8,000,000 |
| 2017 | $12,000,000 |
| 2018 | $15,000,000 |
| 2019 | $10,000,000 |
| 2020 | $12,000,000 |

Equipment, supplies, and salaries were the only three categories for which the bureau spent money.

Candidates may find it useful to arrange their computations on their scratch paper in an orderly manner since the correct computations for one question may also be helpful in answering another question.

1. The information contained in the chart and table is sufficient to determine the     1._____
   - A. average annual salary of an employee in the bureau in 2017
   - B. decrease in the amount of money spent on supplies in the bureau in 2016 from the amount spent in the preceding year
   - C. changes between 2018 and 2019 in the prices of supplies bought by the bureau
   - D. increase in the amount of money spent on salaries in the bureau in 2020 over the amount spent in the preceding year

2. If the percentage of expenditures for salaries in one year is added to the percentage of expenditures for equipment in that year, a total of two percentages for that year is obtained.     2._____
   The two years for which this total is the SAME are
   - A. 2016 and 2018
   - B. 2017 and 2019
   - C. 2016 and 2019
   - D. 2017 and 2020

3. Of the following, the year in which the bureau spent the GREATEST amount of money on supplies was     3._____
   - A. 2020
   - B. 2018
   - C. 2016
   - D. 2016

4. Of the following years, the one in which there was the GREATEST increase over the preceding year in the amount of money spent on salaries is     4._____
   - A. 2019
   - B. 2020
   - C. 2016
   - D. 2018

5. Of the bureau's expenditures for equipment in 2020, one-third was used for the purchase of mailroom equipment and the remainder was spent on miscellaneous office equipment.     5._____
   How much did the bureau spend on miscellaneous office equipment in 2020?
   - A. $4,000,000
   - B. $400,000
   - C. $8,000,000
   - D. $800,000

6. If there were 120 employees in the bureau in 2019, then the average annual salary paid to the employees in that year was MOST NEARLY     6._____
   - A. $43,450
   - B. $49,600
   - C. $58,350
   - D. $80,800

7. In 2018, the bureau had 125 employees.     7._____
   If 20 of the employees earned an average annual salary of $80,000, then the average salary of the other 105 employees was MOST NEARLY
   - A. $49,000
   - B. $64,000
   - C. $41,000
   - D. $54,000

8.  Assume that the bureau estimated that the amount of money it would spend on supplies in 2021 would be the same as the amount it spent on that category in 2020.  Similarly, the bureau estimated that the amount of money it would spend on equipment in 2021 would be the same as the amount it spent on that category in 2020.  However, the bureau estimated that in 2021 the amount it would spend on salaries would be 10 percent higher than the amount it spent on that category in 2020.
The percentage of its annual expenditures that the bureau estimated it would spend on supplies in 2021 is MOST NEARLY
     A.  27.5%        B.  23.5%        C.  22.5%        D.  25%

8.____

____

## KEY (CORRECT ANSWERS)

| | | | |
|---|---|---|---|
| 1. | D | 5. | D |
| 2. | A | 6. | C |
| 3. | B | 7. | A |
| 4. | C | 8. | B |

____

# READING COMPREHENSION
# UNDERSTANDING AND INTERPRETING WRITTEN MATERIAL
## EXAMINATION SECTION
## TEST 1

DIRECTIONS: Each question or incomplete statement is followed by several suggested answers or completions. Select the one that BEST answers the question or completes the statement. *PRINT THE LETTER OF THE CORRECT ANSWER IN THE SPACE AT THE RIGHT.*

Questions 1-4.

DIRECTIONS: Questions 1 through 4 are to be answered SOLELY on the basis of the following paragraph.

An annual leave allowance, which combines leaves previously given for vacation, personal business, family illness, and other reasons shall be granted members. Calculation of credits for such leave shall be on an annual basis beginning January 1ˢᵗ of each year. Annual leave credits shall be based on time served by members during preceding calendar year. However, when credits have been accrued and member retires during current year, additional annual leave credits shall, in this instance, be granted at accrual rate of three days for each completed month of service, excluding terminal leave. If accruals granted for completed months of service extend into following month, member shall be granted an additional three days accrual for completed month. This shall be the only condition where accruals in a current year are granted for vacation period in such year.

1.  According to the above paragraph, if a fireman's wife were to become seriously ill       1.____
    so that he would take time off from work to be with her, such time off would be
    deducted from his _____ leave allowance.
    A. annual                          B. vacation
    C. personal business               D. family illness

2.  Terminal leave means leave taken                                                          2.____
    A. at the end of the calendar year
    B. at the end of the vacation year
    C. immediately before retirement
    D. before actually earned, because of an emergency

3.  A fireman appointed on July 1, 2017 will be able to take his first full or normal         3.____
    annual leave during the period
    A. July 1, 2017 to June 30, 2018      B. Jan. 1, 2018 to Dec. 31, 2018
    C. July 1, 2018 to June 30, 2019      D. Jan. 1, 2019 to Dec. 31, 2019

4.  According to the above paragraph, a member who retires on July 15 of this                 4.____
    year will be entitled to receive leave allowance based on this year of _____ days.
    A. 15          B. 18          C. 22          D. 24

5. Fire alarm boxes are electromechanical devices for transmitting a coded signal. In each box, there is a trainwork of wheels. When the box is operated, a spring-activated code wheel begins to revolve. The code number of the box is etched on the circumference of the code wheel, and the latter is associated with the circuit in such a way that when it revolves it causes the circuit to open and close in a predetermined manner, thereby transmitting its particular signal to the central station. A fire alarm box is nothing more than a device for interrupting the flow of current in a circuit in such a way as to produce a coded signal that may be decoded by the dispatchers in the central office.
Based on the above, select the FALSE statement.
   A. Each standard fire alarm box has its own code wheel.
   B. The code wheel operates when the box is pulled.
   C. The code wheel is operated electrically.
   D. Only the break in the circuit by the notched wheel causes the alarm signal to be transmitted to the central office.

5.\_\_\_\_

Questions 6-9.

DIRECTIONS:   Questions 6 through 9 are to be answered SOLELY on the basis of the following paragraph.

Ventilation, as used in firefighting operations, means opening up a building or structure in which a fire is burning to release the accumulated heat, smoke, and gases. Lack of knowledge of the principles of ventilation on the part of firemen may result in unnecessary punishment due to ventilation being neglected or improperly handled. While ventilation itself extinguishes no fires, when used in an intelligent manner, it allows firemen to get at the fire more quickly, easily, and with less danger and hardship.

6. According to the above paragraph, the MOST important result of failure to apply the principles of ventilation at a fire may be
   A. loss of public confidence      B. waste of water
   C. excessive use of equipment      D. injury to firemen

6.\_\_\_\_

7. It may be inferred from the above paragraph that the CHIEF advantage of ventilation is that it
   A. eliminates the need for gas masks
   B. reduces smoke damage
   C. permits firemen to work closer to the fire
   D. cools the fire

7.\_\_\_\_

8. Knowledge of the principles of ventilation, as defined in the above paragraph, would be LEAST important in a fire in a
   A. tenement house      B. grocery store
   C. ship's hold      D. lumberyard

8.\_\_\_\_

9. We may conclude from the above paragraph that for the well-trained and equipped fireman, ventilation is
   A. a simple matter      B. rarely necessary
   C. relatively unimportant      D. a basic tool

9.\_\_\_\_

Questions 10-13.

DIRECTIONS:   Questions 10 through 13 are to be answered SOLELY on the basis of the
following passage.

Fire exit drills should be established and held periodically to effectively train personnel to leave their working area promptly upon proper signal and to evacuate the building, speedily but without confusion.  All fire exit drills should be carefully planned and carried out in a serious manner under rigid discipline so as to provide positive protection in the event of a real emergency.  As a general rule, the local fire department should be furnished advance information regarding the exact date and time the exit drill is scheduled.  When it is impossible to hold regular drills, written instructions should be distributed to all employees.

Depending upon individual circumstances, fires in warehouses vary from those of fast development that are almost instantly beyond any possibility of employee control to others of relatively slow development where a small readily attackable flame may be present for periods of time up to 15 minutes or more during which simple attack with fire extinguishers or small building hoses may prevent the fire development.  In any case, it is characteristic of many warehouse fires that at a certain point in development they flash up to the top of the stack, increase heat quickly, and spread rapidly.  There is a degree of inherent danger in attacking warehouse type fires, and all employees should be thoroughly trained in the use of the types of extinguishers or small hoses in the buildings and well instructed in the necessity of always staying between the fire and a direct pass to an exit.

10.  Employees should be instructed that, when fighting a fire, they MUST          10._____
A.  try to control the blaze
B.  extinguish any fire in 15 minutes
C.  remain between the fire and a direct passage to the exit
D.  keep the fire between themselves and the fire exit

11.  Whenever conditions are such that regular fire drills cannot be held, then which     11._____
one of the following actions should be taken?
A.  The local fire department should be notified.
B.  Rigid discipline should be maintained during work hours.
C.  Personnel should be instructed to leave their working area by whatever
means are available.
D.  Employees should receive fire drill procedures in writing.

12.  The above passage indicates that the purpose of fire exit drills is to train          12._____
employees to
A.  control a fire before it becomes uncontrollable
B.  act as firefighters
C.  leave the working area promptly
D.  be serious

13. According to the above passage, fire exit drills will prove to be of UTMOST    13._____
effectiveness if
   A. employee participation is made voluntary
   B. they take place periodically
   C. the fire department actively participates
   D. they are held without advance planning

Questions 14-16.

DIRECTIONS:   Questions 14 through 16 are to be answered SOLELY on the basis of the
following paragraph.

The heat output from unit heaters will depend on how fast and how completely dry hot
steam fills the unit core.  For complete and fast air removal and rapid drainage of condensate,
use a trap actuated by water or vapor (inverted bucket trap) and not a trap operated by
temperature only (thermostatic or bellows trap).  A temperature-actuated trap will hold back the
hot condensate until it cools to a point where the thermal element opens.  When this happens,
the condensate backs up in the heater and reduces the heat output.  With a water-actuated trap,
this will not happen as the water or condensate is discharged as fast as it is formed.

14. On the basis of the information given in the above paragraph, it can be    14._____
concluded that the PROPER type of trap to use for a unit heater is a(n) _____
trap.
   A. thermostatic          B  bellows-type
   C. inverted bucket       D. temperature

15. According to the above paragraph, the MAIN reason for using the type of trap    15._____
specified for a unit heater is to
   A. bring the condensate up to steam temperature
   B. prevent reduction in the heat output of the unit heater
   C. permit cycling of the heater
   D. maintain constant temperature of condensate in the trap

16. As used in the above paragraph, the word *actuated* means MOST NEARLY    16._____
   A. clogged      B. operated      C. cleaned      D. vented

Questions 17-25.

DIRECTIONS:   Questions 17 through 25 are to be answered SOLELY on the basis of the
following passage.  Each question consists of a statement.  You are to indicate
whether the statement is TRUE (T) or FALSE (F).

### MOVING AN OFFICE

An office with all its equipment is sometimes moved during working hours.  This is a
difficult task and must be done in an orderly manner to avoid confusion.  The operation should
be planned in such a way as not to interrupt the progress of work usually done in the office and
to make possible the accurate placement of the furniture and records in the new location.  If the
office moves to a place inside the same building, the desks and files are moved with all their

contents. If the movement is to another building, the contents of each desk and file are placed in boxes. Each box is marked with a letter showing the particular section in the new quarters to which it is to be moved. Also marked on each box is the number of the desk or file on which the box is to be placed. Each piece of equipment must have a numbered tag. The number of each piece of equipment is put in soft chalk on the floor in the new office to show the proper location, and several floor plans are made to show where each piece of equipment goes. When the moving is done, someone is stationed at each of the several exits of the old office to see that each box or piece of equipment has its destination clearly marked on it. At the new office, someone stands at each of the several entrances with a copy of the floor plan and directs the placing of the furniture and equipment according to the floor plan. No one should interfere at this point with the arrangements shown on the plan. Improvements in arrangement can be considered and made at a later date.

17. It is a hard job to move an office from one place to another during working hours.     17.____

18. Confusion cannot be avoided if an office is moved during working hours.     18.____

19. The work usually done in an office must be stopped for the day when the office is moved during working hours.     19.____

20. If an office is moved from one floor to another in the same building, the contents of a desk are taken out and put into boxes for moving.     20.____

21. If boxes are used to hold material from desks when moving an office, the box is numbered the same as the desk on which it is to be put.     21.____

22. Letters are marked in soft chalk on the floor at the new quarters to show where the desks should go when moved.     22.____

23. When the moving begins, a person is put at each exit of the old office to check that each box and piece of equipment has clearly marked on it where to go.     23.____

24. A person stationed at each entrance of the new quarters to direct the placing of the furniture and equipment has a copy of the floor plan of the new quarters.     24.____

25. If, while the furniture is being moved into the new office, a person helping at a doorway gets an idea of a better way to arrange the furniture, he should change the planned arrangement and make a record of the change.     25.____

———————

# KEY (CORRECT ANSWERS)

| | | | | |
|---|---|---|---|---|
| 1. | A | | 11. | D |
| 2. | C | | 12. | C |
| 3. | D | | 13. | B |
| 4. | B | | 14. | C |
| 5. | C | | 15. | B |
| | | | | |
| 6. | D | | 16. | B |
| 7. | C | | 17. | T |
| 8. | D | | 18. | F |
| 9. | D | | 19. | F |
| 10. | C | | 20. | F |

| | |
|---|---|
| 21. | T |
| 22. | F |
| 23. | T |
| 24. | T |
| 25. | F |

---

# TEST 2

DIRECTIONS: Each question or incomplete statement is followed by several suggested answers or completions. Select the one that BEST answers the question or completes the statement. *PRINT THE LETTER OF THE CORRECT ANSWER IN THE SPACE AT THE RIGHT.*

Questions 1-4.

DIRECTIONS: Questions 1 through 4 are to be answered SOLELY on the basis of the following paragraph.

In all cases of homicide, members of the Police Department who investigate will make every effort to obtain statements from dying persons. Such statements are of the greatest importance to the District Attorney. In many cases, there may be a failure to solve the crime if they are not taken. The principal element to be considered in taking the declaration of a dying person is his mental attitude. In order to be admissible in evidence, the person must have no hope of recovery. The patient will be fully interrogated on that point before a statement is taken.

1. In cases of homicide, according to the above paragraph, members of the police force will
   A. try to change the mental attitude of the dying person
   B. attempt to obtain a statement from the dying person
   C. not give the information they obtain directly to the District Attorney
   D. be careful not to injure the dying person unnecessarily

   1.____

2. The mental attitude of the person making the dying statement is of GREAT importance because it can determine, according to the above paragraph, whether the
   A. victim should be interrogated in the presence of witnesses
   B. victim will be willing to make a statement of any kind
   C. statement will tell the District Attorney who committed the crime
   D. the statement can be used as evidence

   2.____

3. District Attorneys find that statements of a dying person are important, according to the above paragraph, because
   A. it may be that the victim will recover and then refuse to testify
   B. they are important elements in determining the mental attitude of the victim
   C. they present a point of view
   D. it may be impossible to punish the criminal without such a statement

   3.____

4. A well-known gangster is found dying from a bullet wound. The patrolman first on the scene, in the presence of witnesses, tells the man that he is going to die and asks, *Who shot you?* The gangster says, *Jones shot me, but he hasn't killed me. I'll live to get him.* He then falls back dead.
   According to the above paragraph, this statement is
   A. *admissible* in evidence; the man was obviously speaking the truth
   B. *not admissible* in evidence; the man obviously did not believe that he was dying

   4.____

C. *admissible* in evidence; there were witnesses to the statement
D. *not admissible* in evidence; the victim did not sign any statement and the evidence is merely hearsay

Questions 5-7.

DIRECTIONS:   Questions 5 through 7 are to be answered SOLELY on the basis of the following paragraph.

The factors contributing to crime and delinquency are varied and complex. The home and its immediate environment have been found to be crucial in determining the behavior patterns of the individual, and criminality can frequently be traced to faulty family relationships and a bad neighborhood. But in the search for a clearer understanding of the underlying causes of delinquent and criminal behavior, the total environment must be taken into consideration.

5.   According to the above paragraph, family relationships                                    5.____
    A. tend to become faulty in bad neighborhoods
    B. are important in determining the actions of honest people as well as criminals
    C. are the only important element in the understanding of causes of delinquency
    D. are determined by the total environment

6.   According to the above paragraph, the causes of crime and delinquency are          6.____
    A. not simple                          B. not meaningless
    C. meaningless                         D. simple

7.   According to the above paragraph, faulty family relationships FREQUENTLY         7.____
are
    A. responsible for varied and complex results
    B. caused when one or both parents have a criminal behavior pattern
    C. independent of the total environment
    D. the cause of criminal acts

Questions 8-10.

DIRECTIONS:   Questions 8 through 10 are to be answered SOLELY on the basis of the following paragraph.

A change in the specific problems which confront the police and in the methods for dealing with them has taken place in the last few decades. The automobile is a two-way symbol of this change in policing. It menaces every city with a complicated traffic problem and has speeded up the process of committing a crime and making a getaway, but at the same time has increased the effectiveness of police operations. However, the major concern of police departments continues to be the antisocial or criminal actions and behavior of human beings.

8. On the basis of the above paragraph, it can be stated that, for the most part, in the past few decades the specific problems of a police force
    A. have changed but the general problems have not
    B. as well as the general problems have changed
    C. have remained the same but the general problems have changed
    D. as well as the general problems have remained the same

8._____

9. According to the above paragraph, advances in science and industry have, in general, made the police
    A. operations less effective from the overall point of view
    B. operations more effective from the overall point of view
    C. abandon older methods of solving police problems
    D. concern themselves more with the antisocial acts of human beings

9._____

10. The automobile is a *two-way symbol*, according to the above paragraph, because its use
    A. has speeded up getting to and away from the scene of a crime
    B. both helps and hurts police operations
    C. introduces a new antisocial act—traffic violation—and does away with criminals like horse thieves
    D. both increases and decreases speed by introducing traffic problems

10._____

Questions 11-14.

DIRECTIONS:   Questions 11 through 14 are to be answered SOLELY on the basis of the following passage on INSTRUCTIONS TO COIN AND TOKEN CASHIERS.

## INSTRUCTIONS TO COIN AND TOKEN CASHIERS

Cashiers should reset the machine registers to an even starting number before commencing the day's work. Money bags received directly from collecting agents shall be counted and receipted for on the collecting agent's form. Each cashier shall be responsible for all coin or token bags accepted by him. He must examine all bags to be used for bank deposits for cuts and holes before placing them in use. Care must be exercised so that bags are not cut in opening them. Each bag must be opened separately and verified before another bag is opened. The machine register must be cleared before starting the count of another bag. The amount shown on the machine register must be compared with the amount on the bag tag. The empty bag must be kept on the table for re-examination should there be a difference between the amount on the bag tag and the amount on the machine register.

11. A cashier should BEGIN his day's assignment by
    A. counting and accepting all money bags
    B. resetting the counting machine register
    C. examining all bags for cuts and holes
    D. verifying the contents of all money bags

11._____

12. In verifying the amount of money in the bags received from the collecting agent, it is BEST to
    A. check the amount in one bag at a time
    B. base the total on the amount on the collecting agent's form
    C. repeat the total shown on the bag tag
    D. refer to the bank deposit receipt

12.____

13. A cashier is instructed to keep each empty coin bag on his table while verifying its contents CHIEFLY because, as long as the bag is on the table
    A. it cannot be misplaced
    B. the supervisor can see how quickly the cashier works
    C. cuts and holes are easily noticed
    D. a recheck is possible in case the machine count disagrees with the bag tag total

13.____

14. The INSTRUCTIONS indicate that it is NOT proper procedure for a cashier to
    A. assume that coin bags are free of cuts and holes
    B. compare the machine register total with the total shown on the bag tag
    C. sign a form when he receives coin bags
    D. reset the machine register before starting the day's counting

14.____

Questions 15-17.

DIRECTIONS: Questions 15 through 17 are to be answered SOLELY on the basis of the following passage.

The mass media are an integral part of the daily life of virtually every American. Among these media the youngest, television, is the most pervasive. Ninety-five percent of American homes have at least one T.V. set, and on the average that set is in use for about 40 hours each week. The central place of television in American life makes this medium the focal point of a growing national concern over the effects of media portrayals of violence on the values, attitudes, and behavior of an ever-increasing audience.

In our concern about violence and its causes, it is easy to make television a scapegoat. But we emphasize the fact that there is no simple answer to the problem of violence—no single explanation of its causes, and no single prescription for its control. It should be remembered that America also experienced high levels of crime and violence in periods before the advent of television.

The problem of balance, taste and artistic merit in entertaining programs on television are complex. We cannot countenance government censorship of television. Nor would we seek to impose arbitrary limitations on programming which might jeopardize television's ability to deal in dramatic presentations with controversial social issues. Nonetheless, we are deeply troubled by television's constant portrayal of violence, not in any genuine attempt to focus artistic expression on the human condition, but rather in pandering to a public preoccupation with violence that television itself has helped to generate,

15. According to the above passage, television uses violence MAINLY
    A. to highlight the reality of everyday existence
    B. to satisfy the audience's hunger for destructive action

15.____

C. to shape the values and attitudes of the public
D. when it films documentaries concerning human conflict

16. Which one of the following statements is BEST supported by the above passage?  16.____
    A. Early American history reveals a crime pattern which is not related to television.
    B. Programs should give presentations of social issues and never portray violent acts.
    C. Television has proven that entertainment programs can easily make the balance between taste and artistic merit a simple matter.
    D. Values and behavior should be regulated by governmental censorship.

17. Of the following, which word has the same meaning as *countenance*, as used in  17.____
    the above passage?
    A. Approve       B. Exhibit       C. Oppose       D. Reject

Questions 18-21.

DIRECTIONS:   Questions 18 through 21 are to be answered SOLELY on the basis of the following passage.

    Maintenance of leased or licensed areas on public parks or land has always been a problem.  A good rule to follow in the administration and maintenance of such areas is to limit the responsibility of any lessee or licensee to the maintenance of the structures and grounds essential to the efficient operation of the concession, not including areas for the general use of the public, such as picnic areas, public comfort stations, etc.; except where such facilities are leased to another public agency or where special conditions make such inclusion practicable, and where a good standard of maintenance can be assured and enforced.  If local conditions and requirements are such that public use areas are included, adequate safeguards to the public should be written into contracts and enforced in their administration, to insure that maintenance by the concessionaire shall be equal to the maintenance standards for other park property.

18. According to the above passage, when an area on a public park is leased to a  18.____
    concessionaire, it is usually BEST to
    A. confine the responsibility of the concessionaire to operation of the facilities and leave the maintenance function to the park agency
    B. exclude areas of general public use from the maintenance obligation of the concessionaire
    C. make the concessionaire responsible for maintenance of the entire area including areas of general public use
    D. provide additional comfort station facilities for the area

19. According to the above passage, a valid reason for giving a concessionaire  19.____
    responsibility for maintenance of a picnic area within his leased area is that
    A. local conditions and requirements make it practicable
    B. more than half of the picnic area falls within his leased area
    C. the concessionaire has leased picnic facilities to another public agency
    D. the picnic area falls entirely within his leased area

20. According to the above passage, a precaution that should be taken when a concessionaire is made responsible for maintenance of an area of general public use in a park is
    A. making sure that another public agency has not previously been made responsible for this area
    B. providing the concessionaire with up-to-date equipment, if practicable
    C. requiring that the concessionaire take out adequate insurance for the protection of the public
    D. writing safeguards to the public into the contract

20.____

# KEY (CORRECT ANSWERS)

| | | | |
|---|---|---|---|
| 1. | B | 11. | B |
| 2. | D | 12. | A |
| 3. | D | 13. | D |
| 4. | B | 14. | A |
| 5. | B | 15. | B |
| 6. | A | 16. | A |
| 7. | D | 17. | A |
| 8. | A | 18. | B |
| 9. | B | 19. | A |
| 10. | B | 20. | D |

# TEST 3

DIRECTIONS: Each question or incomplete statement is followed by several suggested answers or completions. Select the one that BEST answers the question or completes the statement. *PRINT THE LETTER OF THE CORRECT ANSWER IN THE SPACE AT THE RIGHT.*

Questions 1-5.

DIRECTIONS: Questions 1 through 5 are to be answered SOLELY on the basis of the following paragraph.

Physical inspections are an important tool for the examiner because he will have to decide the case in many instances on the basis of the inspection report. Most proceedings in a rent office are commenced by the filing of a written application or complaint by an interested party; that is, either the landlord or the tenant. Such an application or complaint must be filed in duplicate in order that the opposing party may be served with a copy of the application or complaint and thus be given an opportunity to answer and oppose it. Sometimes, a further opportunity is given the applicant to file a written rebuttal or reply to his adversary's answer. Often an examiner can make a determination or decision based on the written application, the answer, and the reply to the answer; and, of course, it would speed up operations if it were always possible to make decisions based on written documents only. Unfortunately, decisions can't always be made that way. There are numerous occasions where disputed issues of fact remain which cannot be resolved on the basis of the written statements of the parties. Typical examples are the following: The tenant claims that the refrigerator or stove or bathroom fixture is not functioning properly and the landlord denies this It is obvious that in such cases an inspection of the accommodations is almost the only means of resolving such disputed issues,

1. According to the above paragraph,
   A. physical inspections are made in all cases
   B. physical inspections are seldom made
   C. it is sometimes possible to determine the facts in a case without a physical inspection
   D. physical inspections are made when it is necessary to verify the examiner's determination

1.____

2. According to the above paragraph, in MOST cases, proceedings are started by a(n)
   A. inspector discovering a violation
   B. oral complaint by a tenant or landlord
   C. request from another agency, such as the Building Department
   D. written complaint by a tenant or landlord

2.____

3. According to the above paragraph, when a tenant files an application with the rent office, the landlord is
   A. not told about the proceeding until after the examiner makes his determination
   B. given the duplicate copy of the application

3.____

C. notified by means of an inspector visiting the premises
D. not told about the proceeding until after the inspector has visited the premises

4. As used in the above paragraph, the word *disputed* means MOST NEARLY       4.____
   A. unsettled       B. contested       C. definite       D. difficult

5. As used in the above paragraph, the word *resolved* means MOST NEARLY       5.____
   A. settled       B. fixed       C. helped       D. amended

Questions 6-10.

DIRECTIONS:   Questions 6 through 10 are to be answered SOLELY on the basis of the
              following paragraph.

The examiner should order or request an inspection of the housing accommodations. His request for a physical inspection should be in writing, identify the accommodations and the landlord and the tenant, and specify precisely just what the inspector is to look for and report on. Unless this request is specific and lists in detail every item which the examiner wishes to be reported, the examiner will find that the inspection has not served its purpose and that even with the inspector's report, he is still in no position to decide the case due to loose ends which have not been completely tied up. The items that the examiner is interested in should be separately numbered on the inspection request and the same number referred to in the inspector's report. You can see what it would mean if an inspector came back with a report that did not cover everything. It may mean a tremendous waste of time and often require a re-inspection.

6. According to the above paragraph, the inspector makes an inspection on the       6.____
   order of
   A. the landlord       B. the tenant
   C. the examiner       D. both the landlord and the tenant

7. According to the above paragraph, the reason for numbering each item that       7.____
   an inspector reports on is so that
   A. the report is neat
   B. the report can be easily read and referred to
   C. none of the examiner's requests for information is missed
   D. the report will be specific

8. The one of the following items that is NOT necessarily included in the request       8.____
   for inspection is
   A. location of dwelling       B. name of landlord
   C. item to be checked       D. type of building

9. As used in the above paragraph, the word *precisely* means MOST NEARLY       9.____
   A. exactly       B. generally       C. usually       D. strongly

10. As used in the above paragraph, the words *in detail* mean MOST NEARLY       10.____
    A. clearly       B. item by item       C. substantially       D. completely

Questions 11-13.

DIRECTIONS:   Questions 11 through 13 are to be answered SOLELY on the basis of the
following passage.

The agreement under which a tenant rents property from a landlord is known as a lease.
Generally speaking, leases are classified as either short-term or long-term in duration.  They are
further subdivided according to the method used to determine the amount of periodic rent
payments.  Of the following types of lease in use, the more commonly used ones are the
following:
1.  The straight or fixed lease is one in which rent may be paid in equal amounts
throughout the duration of the lease.  These are usually restricted to short-term
leasing, or somewhat longer-term if clauses in the lease provide for periodic escalation
of payments as the economy shifts.
2.  Percentage leasing, used for short-term commercial leasing, provides the landlord with
a stipulated percentage of a tenant's gross sales from goods and services sold on the
premises, in addition to a fixed amount of rent.
3.  The net lease, generally long-term (ten years or more), requires the tenant to pay all
operating costs, including real estate taxes and insurance.  In a net-net lease, the
tenant further agrees to meet mortgage interest and principal payments.
4.  An escalated lease, which is a long-term lease, requires rent to be of a stipulated base
amount which periodically is subject to escalation in accordance with cost-of-living
index scales, or in direct proportion to taxes, insurance, and operating costs.

11.   Based on the information given in the passage, which type of lease is MOST          11.____
likely to be advantageous to a landlord if there is a high rate of inflation?
_____ lease.
   A.  Fixed          B.  Percentage    C.  Net          D.  Escalated

12.   On the basis of thee above passage, which types of lease would generally be          12.____
MOST suitable for a well-established textile company which requires
permanent facilities for its large operations?
_____ lease and _____ lease.
   A.  Percentage; escalated          B.  Escalated; net
   C.  Straight; net                  D.  Straight; percentage

13.   According to the above passage, the ONLY type of lease which assures the          13.____
same amount of rent throughout a specified interval is the _____ lease.
   A.  straight          B.  percentage    C.  net-net          D.  escalated

Questions 14-15.

DIRECTIONS:   Questions 14 and 15 are to be answered SOLELY on the basis of the following
passage.

If you like people, if you seek contact with them rather than hide yourself in a corner, if you study your fellow men sympathetically, if you try consistently to contribute something to their success and happiness, if you are reasonably generous with your thought and your time, if you have a partial reserve with everyone but a seeming reserve with no one, you will get along with your superiors, your subordinates, and the human race.

By the scores of thousands, precepts and platitudes have been written for the guidance of personal conduct. The odd part of it is that, despite all of this labor, most of the frictions in modern society arise from the individual's feeling of inferiority, his false pride, his vanity, his unwillingness to yield space to any other man and his consequent urge to throw his own weight around. Goethe said that the quality which best enables a man to renew his own life, in his relation to others, is his capability of renouncing particular things at the right moment in order warmly to embrace something new in the next.

14. On the basis of the above passage, it may be INFERRED that             14.____
    A. a person should be unwilling to renounce privileges
    B. a person should realize that loss of a desirable job assignment may come at an opportune moment
    C. it is advisable for a person to maintain a considerable amount of reserve in his relationship with unfamiliar people
    D. people should be ready to contribute generously to a worthy charity

15. Of the following, the MOST valid implication made by the above passage is that     15.____
    A. a wealthy person who spends a considerable amount of money entertaining his friends is not really getting along with them
    B. if a person studies his fellow men carefully and impartially, he will tend to have good relationships with them
    C. individuals who maintain seemingly little reserve in their relationships with people have in some measure overcome their own feelings of inferiority
    D. most precepts that have been written for the guidance of personal conduct in relationships with other people are invalid

Questions 16-17.

DIRECTIONS:   Questions 16 and 17 are to be answered SOLELY on the basis of the following passage.

When a design for a new bank note of the Federal Government has been prepared by the Bureau of Engraving and Printing and has been approved by the Secretary of the Treasury, the engravers begin the work of cutting the design in steel. No one engraver does all the work. Each man is a specialist. One works only on portraits, another on lettering, another on scroll work, and so on. Each engraver, with a steel tool known as a graver, and aided by a powerful magnifying glass, carefully carves his portion of the design into the steel. He knows that one false cut or a slip of his tool, or one miscalculation of width or depth of line, may destroy the merit of his work. A single mistake means that months or weeks of labor will have been in vain. The bureau is proud of the fact that no counterfeiter ever has duplicated the excellent work of its expert engravers.

16. According to the above passage, each engraver in the Bureau of Engraving and Printing      16.____
   A. must be approved by the Secretary of the Treasury before he can begin work on the design for a new bank note
   B. is responsible for engraving a complete design of a new bank note by himself
   C. designs new bank notes and submits them for approval to the Secretary of the Treasury
   D. performs sonly a specific part of the work of engraving a design for a new bank note

17. According to the above passage,      17.____
   A. an engraver's tools are not available to a counterfeiter
   B. mistakes made in engraving a design can be corrected immediately with little delay in the work of the Bureau
   C. the skilled work of the engravers has not been successfully reproduced by counterfeiter
   D. careful carving and cutting by the engraver is essential to prevent damage to equipment

Questions 18-21.

DIRECTIONS: Questions 18 through 21 are to be answered SOLELY on the basis of the following passage.

In the late fifties, the average American housewife spent $4.50 per day for a family of four on food and 5.15 hours in food preparation, if all of her food was *home prepared*; she spent $5.80 per day and 3.245 hours if all of her food was purchased *partially prepared*; and $6.70 per day and 1.64 hours if all of her food was purchased *ready-to-serve*.

Americans spent about 20 billion dollars for food products in 1941. They spent nearly 70 billion dollars in 1958. They spent 25 percent of their cash income on food in 1958. For the same kinds and quantities of food that consumers bought in 1941, they would have spent only 16% of their cash income in 1958. It is obvious that our food does cost more. Many factors contribute to this increase besides the additional cost that might be attributed to processing. Consumption of more expensive food items, higher marketing margins, and more food eaten in restaurants are other factors.

The Census of Manufacturers gives some indication of the total bill for processing. The value added by manufacturing of food and kindred products amounted to 3.5 billion of the 20 billion dollars spent for food in 1941. In the year 1958, the comparable figure had climbed to 14 billion dollars.

18. According to the above passage, the cash income of Americans in 1958 was MOST NEARLY _____ billion dollars.      18.____
   A. 11.2       B. 17.5       C. 70       D. 280

19. According to the above passage, if Americans bought the same kinds and quantities of food in 1958 as they did in 1941, they would have spent MOST NEARLY _____ billion dollars.      19.____
   A. 20       B. 45       C. 74       D. 84

20. According to the above passage, the percent increase in money spent for food     20._____
in 1958 over 1941, as compared with the percentage increase in money spent
for food processing in the same years,
   A. was greater
   B. was less
   C. was the same
   D. cannot be determined from the passage

21. In 1958, an American housewife who bought all of her food ready-to-serve saved     21._____
time, as compared with the housewife who prepared all of her food at home
   A. 1.6 hours daily
   B. 1.9 hours daily
   C. 3.5 hours daily
   D. an amount of time which cannot be determined from the above passage

Questions 22-25.

DIRECTIONS:   Questions 22 through 25 are to be answered SOLELY on the basis of the
following passage.

Any member of the retirement system who is in city service, who files a proper application
for service credit and agrees to deductions from his compensation at triple his normal rate of
contribution, shall be credited with a period of city service previous to the beginning of his
present membership in the retirement system.  The period of service credited shall be equal to
the period throughout which such triple deductions are made, but may not exceed the total of
the city service the number rendered between his first day of eligibility for membership in the
retirement system and the day he last became a member.  After triple contributions for all of the
first three years of service credit claimed, the remaining service credit may be purchased by a
single payment of the sum of the remaining payments.  If the total time purchasable exceeds ten
years, triple contributions may be made for one-half of such time, and the remaining time
purchased by a single payment of the sum of the remaining payments.  Credit for service
acquired in the above manner may be used only in determining the amount of any retirement
benefit.  Eligibility for such benefit will, in all cases, be based upon service rendered after the
employee's membership last began, and will be exclusive of service credit purchased as
described above.

22. According to the above passage, in order to obtain credit for city service     22._____
previous to the beginning of an employee's present membership in the
retirement system, the employee must
   A. apply for the service credit and consent to additional contributions to the
      retirement system
   B. apply for the service credit before he renews his membership in the
      retirement system
   C. have previous city service which does not exceed ten years
   D. make contributions to the retirement system for three years

23. According to the information in the above passage, credit for city service previous to the beginning of an employee's present membership in the retirement system is
    A. credited up to a maximum of ten years
    B. credited to any member of the retirement system
    C. used in determining the amount of the employee's benefits
    D. used in establishing the employee's eligibility to receive benefits

23.____

24. According to the information in the above passage, a member of the retirement system may purchase service credit for
    A. the period of time between his first day of eligibility for membership in the retirement system and the date he applies for the service credit
    B. one-half of the total of his previous city service if the total time exceeds ten years
    C. the period of time throughout which triple deductions are made
    D. the period of city service between his first day of eligibility for membership in the retirement system and the day he last became a member

24.____

25. Suppose that a member of the retirement system has filed an application for service credit for five years of previous city service.
    Based on the information in the above passage, the employee may purchase credit for this previous city service by making
    A. triple contributions for three years
    B. triple contributions for one-half of the time and a single payment of the sum of the remaining payments
    C. triple contributions for three years and a single payment of the sum of the remaining payments
    D. a single payment of the sum of the payments

25.____

# KEY (CORRECT ANSWERS)

| | | | | |
|---|---|---|---|---|
| 1. | C | | 11. | D |
| 2. | D | | 12. | B |
| 3. | B | | 13. | A |
| 4. | B | | 14. | B |
| 5. | A | | 15. | C |
| | | | | |
| 6. | C | | 16. | D |
| 7. | C | | 17. | C |
| 8. | D | | 18. | D |
| 9. | A | | 19. | B |
| 10. | B | | 20. | B |

| | |
|---|---|
| 21. | C |
| 22. | A |
| 23. | C |
| 24. | D |
| 25. | C |

# EXAMINATION SECTION
## TEST 1

DIRECTIONS: Each question or incomplete statement is followed by several suggested answers or completions Select the one that BEST answers the question or completes the statement. *PRINT THE LETTER OF THE CORRECT ANSWER IN THE SPACE AT THE RIGHT.*

1. There is considerable rivalry among employees in a certain department over location of desks. It is the practice of the supervisor to assign desks without any predetermined plan. The supervisor is reconsidering his procedure. In assigning desks, PRIMARY consideration should *ordinarily* be given to
   A. past practices
   B. flow of work
   C. employee seniority
   D. social relations among employees

1.\_\_\_\_\_

2. Assume that, when you tell some of the workers under your supervision that the jobs they prepare   have too many errors, they contend that the performance is sufficient and that they obtain more satisfaction from their jobs if they do not have to be as concerned about errors. These workers are
   A. *correct,* because the ultimate objective should be job satisfaction
   B. *incorrect,* because every job should be performed perfectly
   C. *correct,* because they do not create the jobs themselves
   D. *incorrect,* because their satisfaction is not the only consideration

2.\_\_\_\_\_

3. Which of the following possible conditions is LEAST likely to represent a hindrance to effective  communication?
   A. The importance of a situation may not be apparent.
   B. Words may mean different things to different people.
   C. The recipient of a communication may respond to it, sometimes unfavorably.
   D. Communications may affect the self-interest of those communicating.

3.\_\_\_\_\_

4. You are revising the way in which your unit handles records.  One of the BEST ways to make sure that the change will be implemented with a minimum of difficulty is to
   A. allow everyone on the staff who is affected by the change to have an opportunity to contribute their ideas  to the new procedures
   B. advise only the key members of your staff in advance so that they can help you enforce the new method when it is implemented
   C. give the assignment of implementation to the newest member of the unit
   D. issue a memorandum announcing the change and stating that complaints will not be tolerated

4.\_\_\_\_\_

5. One of your assistants is quite obviously having personal problems that are affecting his work performance.
   As a supervisor, it would be MOST appropriate for you to
   A. avoid any inquiry into the nature of the situation since this is not one of your responsibilities
   B. avoid any discussion of personal problems on the basis that there is nothing you could do about them anyhow
   C. help the employee obtain appropriate help with these problems
   D. advise the employee that personal problems cannot be considered when evaluating work performance

5.\_\_\_\_\_

6. The key to improving communication with your staff and other departments is the development of an awareness of the importance of communication.
Which of the following is NOT a good suggestion for developing this awareness?
   A. Be willing to look at your own attitude toward how you communicate
   B. Be sensitive and receptive to reactions to what you tell people
   C. Make sure all communication is in writing
   D. When giving your subordinates directions, try to put yourself in their place and see if your instructions still make sense

6.\_\_\_\_\_

7. One of the assistants on your staff has neglected to complete an important assignment on schedule. You feel that a reprimand is necessary.
When speaking to the employee, it would *usually* be LEAST desirable to
   A. display your anger to show the employee how strongly you feel about the problem
   B. ask several questions about the reasons for failure to complete the assignment
   C. take the employee aside so that nobody else is present when you discuss the matter
   D. give the employee as much time as he needs to explain exactly what happened

7.\_\_\_\_\_

8. One of the techniques of management often used by supervisors is performance appraisal. Which of the following is NOT one of the objectives of performance appraisal?
   A. Improve staff performance
   B. Determine individual training needs
   C. Improve organizational structure
   D. Set standards and performance criteria for employees

8.\_\_\_\_\_

9. An employee can be motivated to fulfill his needs as he sees them. He is not motivated by what others think he ought to have, but what he himself wants.
Which of the following statements follows MOST logically from the foregoing viewpoint?
   A. A person's different traits may be separately classified, but they are all part of one system comprising a whole person.
   B. Every job, however simple, entitles the person who does it to proper respect and recognition of his unique aspirations and abilities.
   C. No matter what equipment and facilities an organization has, they cannot be put to use except by people who have been motivated.
   D. To an observer, a person's need may be unrealistic but they are still controlling.

9.\_\_\_\_\_

10. When delegating responsibility for an assignment to a subordinate, it is MOST important that you
   A. retain all authority necessary to complete the assignment
   B. make yourself generally available for consultation with the subordinate
   C. inform your superiors that you are no longer responsible for the assignment
   D. decrease the number of subordinates whom you have to supervise

10.\_\_\_\_\_

11. One of the things that can ruin morale in a work group is the failure to exercise judgment in the assignment of overtime work to your subordinates.
Of the following, the MOST desirable supervisory practice in assigning overtime work is to
    A. rotate overtime on a uniform basis among all your subordinates
    B. assign overtime to those who are *moonlighting* after regular work hours
    C. rotate overtime as much as possible among employees willing to work additional hours
    D. assign overtime to those employees who take frequent long weekend vacations

11._____

12. The consistent delegation of authority by you to experienced and reliable subordinates in your work group is GENERALLY considered
    A. *undesirable*, because your authority in the group may be threatened by an unscrupulous subordinate
    B. *undesirable*, because it demonstrates that you cannot handle your own workload
    C. *desirable*, because it shows that you believe that you have been accepted by your subordinates
    D. *desirable*, because the development of subordinates creates opportunities for assuming broader responsibilities yourself

12._____

13. The MOST effective way for you to deal with a false rumor circulating among your subordinates is to
    A. have a trusted subordinate start a counter-rumor
    B. recommend disciplinary action against the *rumor mongers*
    C. point out to your subordinates that rumors degrade both listener and initiator
    D. furnish your subordinates, with sufficient authentic information

13._____

14. Two of your subordinates tell you about a mistake they made in a report that has already been sent to top management.
Which of the following questions is *most likely* to elicit the MOST valuable information from your subordinates?
    A. Who is responsible?
    B. How can we explain this to top management?
    C. How did it happen?
    D. Why weren't you more careful?

14._____

15. Assume that you are responsible for implementing major changes in work flow patterns and personnel assignments in the unit of which you are in charge.
The one of the following actions which is MOST likely to secure the willing cooperation of those persons who will have to change their assignment is
    A. having the top administrators of the agency urge their cooperation at a group meeting
    B. issuing very detailed and carefully planned instructions to the affected employees regarding the changes
    C. integrating employee participation into the planning of the changes
    D. reminding the affected employees that career advancement depends upon compliance with organizational objectives

15._____

16. Of the following, the BEST reason for using face-to-face communication instead of written communication is that face-to-face communication
    A. allows for immediate feedback
    B. is more credible
    C. enables greater use of detail and illustration
    D. is more polite

17. Of the following, the MOST likely disadvantage of giving detailed instructions when assigning a task to a subordinate is that such instructions may
    A. conflict with the subordinate's ideas of how the task should be done
    B. reduce standardization of work performance
    C. cause confusion in the mind of the subordinate
    D. inhibit the development of new procedures by the subordinate

18. Assume that you are a supervisor of a unit consisting of a number of subordinates and that one subordinate, whose work is otherwise acceptable, keeps on making errors in one particular task assigned to him in rotation. This task consists of routine duties which all your subordinates should be able to perform.
    Of the following, the BEST way for you to handle this situation is to
    A. do the task yourself when the erring employee is scheduled to perform it and assign this employee other duties
    B. reorganize work assignments so that the task in question is no longer performed in rotation but assigned full-time to your most capable subordinate
    C. find out why this subordinate keeps on making the errors in question and see that he learns how to 'do the task properly
    D. maintain a well-documented record of such errors and, when the evidence is overwhelming, recommend appropriate disciplinary action

19. It is better for an employee to report and be responsible directly to several supervisors than to report and be responsible to only one supervisor.
    This statement directly CONTRADICTS the supervisory principle *generally* known as
    A. span of control
    B. unity of command
    C. delegation of authority
    D. accountability

20. The one of the following which would MOST likely lead to friction among clerks in a unit is for the unit supervisor to
    A. defend the actions of his clerks when discussing them with his own supervisor
    B. praise each of his clerks in *confidence* as the best clerk in the unit
    C. get his men to work together as a team in completing the work of the unit
    D. consider the point of view of the rank and file clerks when assigning unpleasant tasks

21. You become aware that one of the employees you supervise has failed to follow correct procedure and has been permitting various reports to be prepared, typed, and transmitted improperly.
The BEST action for you to take FIRST in this situation is to
    A. order the employee to review all departmental procedures and reprimand him for having violated them
    B. warn the employee that he must obey regulations because uniformity is essential for effective departmental operation
    C. confer with the employee both about his failure to follow regulations and his reasons for doing so
    D. watch the employee's work very closely in the future but say nothing about this violation

21.\_\_\_\_\_

22. When routine procedures covering the ordinary work of an office are established, the supervisor of the office tends to be relieved of the need to
    A. make repeated decisions on the handling of recurring similar situations
    B. check the accuracy of the work completed by his subordinates
    C. train his subordinates in new work procedures
    D. plan and schedule the work of his office

22.\_\_\_\_\_

23. Of the following, the method which would be LEAST helpful to a supervisor in effectively applying the principles of on-the-job safety to the daily work of his unit is for him to
    A. initiate corrections of unsafe layouts of equipment and unsafe work processes
    B. take charge of operations that are not routine to make certain that safety precautions are established and observed
    C. continue to *talk safety* and promote safety consciousness in his subordinates
    D. figure the cost of all accidents which could possibly occur on the job

23.\_\_\_\_\_

24. A clerk is assigned to serve as receptionist for a large and busy office. Although many members of the public visit this office, the clerk often experiences periods of time in which he has nothing to do.
In these circumstances, the MOST advisable of the following actions for the supervisor to take is to
    A. assign a number of relatively low priority clerical jobs to the receptionist to do in the slow periods
    B. regularly rotate this assignment so that all of the clerks experience this lighter workload
    C. assign the receptionist job as part of the duties of a number of clerks whose desks are nearest the reception room
    D. overlook the situation since most of the receptionist's time is spent in performing a necessary and meaningful function

24.\_\_\_\_\_

25. For a supervisor to require all workers in a gang to produce the same amount of work on a particular day is
    A. *advisable* since it will prove that the supervisor plays no favorites
    B. *fair* since all the workers are receiving approximately the same salary, their output should be equivalent
    C. *not necessary* since the fast workers will compensate for the slow workers
    D. *not realistic* since individual differences in abilities and work assignment must be taken into consideration

25.\_\_\_\_\_

# KEY (CORRECT ANSWERS)

| | | | |
|---|---|---|---|
| 1. B | | 11. C |
| 2. D | | 12. D |
| 3. C | | 13. D |
| 4. A | | 14. C |
| 5. C | | 15. C |
| 6. C | | 16. A |
| 7. A | | 17. D |
| 8. C | | 18. C |
| 9. D | | 19. B |
| 10. B | | 20. B |

21. C
22. A
23. D
24. A
25. D

———

# TEST 2

DIRECTIONS: Each question or incomplete statement is followed by several suggested answers or completions Select the one that BEST answers the question or completes the statement. *PRINT THE LETTER OF THE CORRECT ANSWER IN THE SPACE AT THE RIGHT.*

1. A certain employee has a poor tardiness record and was recently warned by her supervisor that certain disciplinary action would be taken if she were late again. If she comes in late again, in private, the supervisor should

    A. speak to her right away and, after listening to her explanation, impose any warranted discipline quietly and impersonally

    B. speak to her during the next afternoon; this will prevent an emotional confrontation and will give her time to fully realize the consequences of her actions

    C. speak to her right away and make an attempt to soften the necessary disciplinary action by apologizing for having to use discipline

    D. speak to her right away and remind her, in no uncertain terms, of the difficulty she has caused him by her continual lateness before imposing any warranted discipline

1._____

2. Choosing supervisors strictly from within a particular working section GENERALLY is

    A. *desirable*, primarily because the budgeting necessary for promotion is substantially decreased

    B. *undesirable* because personal preferences will always outweigh merit

    C. *desirable*, primarily because a good worker within that section will be a good supervisor for that section alone

    D. *undesirable*, primarily because the pool of candidates will be severely limited

2._____

3. Of the following, a supervisor interested in setting quality standards for work produced by his subordinates PRIMARILY should

    A. consult with supervisors in other organizations to determine the range of acceptable standards

    B. institute a quality improvement program and set standards at the point where quality levels off at desirable levels

    C. establish an ad hoc committee comprised of a representative sample of workers to set firm and exacting standards

    D. consult the QUALITY STANDARDS HANDBOOK which predetermines with mathematical precision the level of quality the work should meet

3._____

4. The supervisor who would be MOST likely to have poor control over his subordinates is the one who

    A. goes to unusually great lengths to try to win their approval

    B. pitches in with the work they are doing during periods of heavy workload when no extra help can be obtained

    C. encourages and helps his subordinates toward advancement

    D. considers suggestions from his subordinates before establishing new work procedures involving them

4._____

5.  Suppose that a clerk who has been transferred to your office from another division     5._____
    in your agency because of difficulties with his supervisor has been placed under
    your supervision.
    The BEST course of action for you to take FIRST is to
    A.  instruct the clerk in the duties he will be performing in your office and make
        him feel *wanted* in his new position
    B.  analyze the clerk's past grievance to determine if the transfer was the best
        solution to the problem
    C.  advise him of the difficulties his former supervisor had with other employees
        and encourage him not to feel bad about the transfer
    D.  warn him that you will not tolerate any nonsense and that he will be under
        continuous surveillance while assigned to you

6.  A certain office supervisor takes the initiative to                                     6._____
    represent his employees' interests related to working conditions, opportunities for
    advancement, etc.  to his own supervisor and the administrative levels of the agency.
    This supervisor's actions will MOST probably have the effect of
    A.  preventing employees from developing individual initiative in their work goals
    B.  encouraging employees to compete openly for the special attention of their
        supervisor
    C.  depriving employees of the opportunity to be represented by persons and/or
        unions of their own choosing
    D.  building employee confidence in their supervisor and a spirit of cooperation
        in their work

7.  Suppose that you have been promoted, assigned as a supervisor of a certain unit,        7._____
    and asked to reorganize its functions so that specific routine procedures can be
    established. Before deciding which routines to establish, the FIRST of the following
    steps you should take is to
    A.  decide who will perform each task in the routine
    B.  determine the purpose to be served by each routine procedure
    C.  outline the sequence of steps in each routine to be established
    D.  calculate if more staff will be needed to carry out the new procedures

8.  The establishment of a centralized typing pool to service the various units in an       8._____
    organization is MOST likely to be worthwhile when there is
    A.  wide fluctuation from time to time in the needs of the various units for
        typing service
    B.  a large volume of typing work to be done in each of the units
    C.  a need by each unit for different kinds of typing service
    D.  a training program in operation to develop and maintain typing skills

9.  A newly appointed supervisor should learn as much as possible about the backgrounds     9._____
    of his subordinates. This statement is GENERALLY correct because
    A.  knowing their backgrounds assures they will be treated objectively, equally,
        and without favor
    B.  effective handling of subordinates is based upon knowledge of their individual
        differences
    C.  subordinates perform more efficiently under one supervisor than under another
    D.  subordinates have confidence in a supervisor who knows all about them

10. The use of electronic computers in modern businesses has produced many changes     10._____
    in office and information management. Of the following, it would NOT be correct to
    state that computer utilization
    A. broadens the scope of managerial and supervisory authority
    B. establishes uniformity in the processing and reporting of information
    C. cuts costs by reducing the personnel needed for efficient office operation
    D. supplies management rapidly with up-to-date data to facilitate decision-making

11. The CHIEF advantage of having a single, large open office instead of small partitioned     11._____
    ones for a clerical unit is that the single, large open office
    A. affords privacy without isolation for all office workers not directly dealing with the
       public
    B. assures the smoother more continuous inter-office flow of work that is essential
       for efficient work production
    C. facilitates the office supervisor's visual control over and communication with his
       subordinates
    D. permits a more decorative and functional arrangement of office furniture and
       machines

12. When a supervisor provides a new employee with the information necessary for a     12._____
    basic knowledge and a general understanding of practices and procedures of the
    agency, he is applying the type of training GENERALLY known as _____training.
    A. pre-employment
    B. induction
    C. on-the-job
    D. supervisory

13. Assume that a large office in a certain organization operates long hours and is thus     13._____
    on two shifts with a slight overlap. Those employees, including supervisors, who are
    most productive are given their choice of shifts. The earlier shift is considered
    preferable by most employees. As a result of this method of assignment, which of
    the following is MOST likely to result?
    A. Most non-supervisory employees will be assigned to the late shift; most
       supervisors will be assigned to the early shift.
    B. Most supervisors will be assigned to the late shift; most non-supervisory
       employees will be assigned to the early shift.
    C. The early shift will be more productive than the late shift.
    D. The late shift will 'be more productive than the early shift.

14. Assume that a supervisor of a unit in which the employees are of average friendliness     14._____
    tells a newly-hired employee on her first day that her co-workers are very friendly.
    The other employees hear his remarks to the new employee. Which of the following is
    the MOST likely result of this action of the supervisor?
    The
    A. newly-hired employee will tend to feel less friendly than if the supervisor had
       said nothing
    B. newly-hired employee will tend to believe that her co-workers are very friendly
    C. other employees will tend to feel less friendly toward one another
    D. other employees will tend to see the newly-hired employee as insincerely friendly

15. A recent study of employee absenteeism showed that, although unscheduled absence for part of a week is relatively high for young employees, unscheduled absence for a full week is low. However, although full-week unscheduled absence is least frequent for the youngest employees, the frequency of such absence increases as the age of employees increase.

    Which of the following statements is the MOST logical explanation for the greater full-week absenteeism among older employees?
    A. Older employees are more likely to be males.
    B. Older employees are more likely to have more relatively serious illnesses.
    C. Younger employees are more likely to take longer vacations.
    D. Younger employees are more likely to be newly-hired.

    15._____

16. Because higher status is important to many employees, they will often make an effort to achieve it as an end in itself.

    Of the following, the BEST course of action for the supervisor to take on the basis of the preceding statement is to
    A. attach higher status to that behavior of subordinates which is directed toward reaching the goals of the organization
    B. avoid showing sympathy toward subordinates' wishes for increased wages, improved working conditions, or other benefits
    C. foster interpersonal competitiveness among subordinates so that personal friendliness is replaced by the desire to protect individual status
    D. reprimand subordinates whenever their work is in some way unsatisfactory in order to adjust their status accordingly

    16._____

17. From the viewpoint of an office supervisor, the BEST of the following reasons for distributing the incoming mail before the beginning of the regular work day is that
    A. distribution can be handled quickly and most efficiently at that time
    B. distribution later in the day may be distracting to or interfere with other employees
    C. the employees who distribute the mail can then perform other tasks during the rest of the day
    D. office activities for the day based on the mail may then be started promptly

    17._____

18. Suppose you are the head of a unit with 10 staff members who are located in several different rooms.

    If you want to inform your staff of a minor change in procedure, the BEST and LEAST expensive way of doing so would *usually* be to
    A. send a mimeographed copy to each staff member
    B. call a special staff meeting and announce the change
    C. circulate a memo, having each staff member initial it
    D. have a clerk tell each member of the staff about the change

    18._____

19. Suppose you are the supervisor of the mailroom of a large city agency where the mail received daily is opened by machine, sorted by hand for delivery, and time-stamped. Letters and any enclosures are removed from envelopes and stapled together before distribution. One of your newest clerks asks you what should be done when a letter makes reference to an enclosure but no enclosure is in the envelope. You should tell him that, in this situation, the BEST procedure is to
    A. make an entry of the sender's name and address in the *missing enclosures* file and forward the letter to its proper destination
    B. return the letter to its sender, attaching a request for the missing enclosure
    C. put the letter aside until a proper investigation may be made concerning the missing enclosure
    D. route the letter to the person for whom it is intended, noting the absence of the enclosure on the letter-margin

    19._____

20. James Jones is applying for a provisional appointment as a clerk in your department. He presents a letter of recommendation from a former employer stating: *James Jones was rarely late or absents he has a very pleasing manner and never got into an argument with his fellow employees.* The above information concerning this applicant
    A. proves clearly that he produces more work than the average employee
    B. indicates that he was probably attempting to conceal his inefficiency from his former employer
    C. presents no conclusive evidence of his ability to do clerical work
    D. indicates clearly that with additional training he will make a good supervisor

    20._____

21. In the past, Mr. T, one of your subordinates, had been generally withdrawn and suspicious of others, but he had produced acceptable work. However, Mr. T has lately started to get into arguments with his fellow workers during which he displays intense rage. Friction between this subordinate and the others in your unit is mounting, and the unit's work is suffering.
Of the following, which would be the BEST way for you to handle this situation?
    A. Rearrange work schedules and assignments so as to give Mr. T no cause for complaint
    B. Instruct the other workers to avoid Mr. T and not to respond to any abuse
    C. Hold a unit meeting and appeal for harmony and submergence of individual differences in the interest of work
    D. Maintain a record of incidents and explore with Mr. T the possibility of seeking professional help

    21._____

22. You are responsible for seeing to it that your unit is functioning properly in the accomplishment of it budgeted goals.
Which of the following will provide the LEAST information on how well you are accomplishing such goals?
    A. Measurement of employee performance
    B. Identification of alternative goals
    C. Detection of employee errors
    D. Preparation of unit reports

    22._____

23. Some employees see an agency training program as a threat. Of the following, the MOST likely reason for such an employee attitude toward training is that the employees involved feel that
    A. some trainers are incompetent
    B. training rarely solves real work-a-day problems
    C. training may attempt to change comfortable behavior patterns
    D. training sessions are boring

    23._____

24. All of the following are correct methods for a supervisor to use in connection with        24._____
    employee discipline EXCEPT
    A. trying not to be too lenient or too harsh
    B. informing employees of the rules and the penalties for violations of the rules
    C. imposing discipline immediately after the violation is discovered
    D. making sure, when you apply discipline, that the employee understands that
       you do not want to do it

25. Of the following, the MAIN reason for a supervisor to establish standard procedures        25._____
    for his unit is to
    A. increase the motivation of his subordinates
    B. make it easier for the subordinates to submit to authority
    C. reduce the number of times that his subordinates have to consult him
    D. reduce the number of mistakes that his subordinates will make

---

# KEY (CORRECT ANSWERS)

| | | |
|---|---|---|
| 1. A | | 11. C |
| 2. D | | 12. B |
| 3. B | | 13. C |
| 4. A | | 14. B |
| 5. A | | 15. B |
| | | |
| 6. D | | 16. A |
| 7. B | | 17. D |
| 8. A | | 18. C |
| 9. B | | 19. D |
| 10. A | | 20. C |

21. D
22. B
23. C
24. D
25. C

---

# PHILOSOPHY, PRINCIPLES, PRACTICES, AND TECHNICS
## OF
## SUPERVISION, ADMINISTRATION, MANAGEMENT, AND ORGANIZATION

## TABLE OF CONTENTS

---

# PHILOSOPHY, PRINCIPLES, PRACTICES, AND TECHNICS
## OF
## SUPERVISION, ADMINISTRATION, MANAGEMENT, AND ORGANIZATION

## MEANING OF SUPERVISION

The extension of the democratic philosophy has been accompanied by an extension in the scope of supervision. Modern leaders and supervisors no longer think of supervision in the narrow sense of being confined chiefly to visiting employees, supplying materials, or rating the staff. They regard supervision as being intimately related to all the concerned agencies of society, they speak of the supervisor's function in terms of "growth," rather than the "improvement" of employees.

This modern concept of supervision may be defined as follows: Supervision is leadership and the development of leadership within groups which are cooperatively engaged in inspection, research, training, guidance, and evaluation.

## THE OLD AND THE NEW SUPERVISION

### TRADITIONAL
1. Inspection
2. Focused on the employee
3. Visitation
4. Random and haphazard
5. Imposed and authoritarian
6. One person usually

### MODERN
1. Study and analysis
2. Focused on aims, materials, methods, supervisors, employees, environment
3. Demonstrations, intervisitation, workshops, directed reading, bulletins, etc.
4. Definitely organized and planned (scientific)
5. Cooperative and democratic
6. Many persons involved (creative)

## THE EIGHT (8) BASIC PRINCIPLES OF THE NEW SUPERVISION

I.  Principle of Responsibility
    Authority to act and responsibility for acting must be joined.
    A. If you give responsibility, give authority.
    B. Define employee duties clearly.
    C. Protect employees from criticism by others.
    D. Recognize the rights as well as obligations of employees.
    E. Achieve the aims of a democratic society insofar as it is possible within the area of your work.
    F. Establish a situation favorable to training and learning.
    G. Accept ultimate responsibility for everything done in your section, unit, office, division, department.
    H. Good administration and good supervision are inseparable.

II.  Principle of Authority
The success of the supervisor is measured by the extent to which the power of authority is not used.
A.  Exercise simplicity and informality in supervision
B.  Use the simplest machinery of supervision
C.  If it is good for the organization as a whole, it is probably justified.
D.  Seldom be arbitrary or authoritative.
E.  Do not base your work on the power of position or of personality.
F.  Permit and encourage the free expression of opinions.

III.  Principle of Self-Growth
The success of the supervisor is measured by the extent to which, and the speed with which, he is no longer needed.
A.  Base criticism on principles, not on specifics.
B.  Point out higher activities to employees.
C.  Train for self-thinking by employees to meet new situations.
D.  Stimulate initiative, self-reliance, and individual responsibility
E.  Concentrate on stimulating the growth of employees rather than on removing defects.

IV.  Principle of Individual Worth
Respect for the individual is a paramount consideration in supervision.
A.  Be human and sympathetic in dealing with employees.
B.  Don't nag about things to be done.
C.  Recognize the individual differences among employees and seek opportunities to permit best expression of each personality.

V.  Principle of Creative Leadership
The best supervision is that which is not apparent to the employee.
A.  Stimulate, don't drive employees to creative action.
B.  Emphasize doing good things.
C.  Encourage employees to do what they do best.
D.  Do not be too greatly concerned with details of subject or method.
E.  Do not be concerned exclusively with immediate problems and activities.
F.  Reveal higher activities and make them both desired and maximally possible.
G.  Determine procedures in the light of each situation but see that these are derived from a sound basic philosophy.
H.  Aid, inspire, and lead so as to liberate the creative spirit latent in all good employees.

VI.  Principle of Success and Failure
There are no unsuccessful employees, only unsuccessful supervisors who have failed to give proper leadership.
A.  Adapt suggestions to the capacities, attitudes, and prejudices of employees.
B.  Be gradual, be progressive, be persistent.
C.  Help the employee find the general principle; have the employee apply his own problem to the general principle.
D.  Give adequate appreciation for good work and honest effort.
E.  Anticipate employee difficulties and help to prevent them.
F.  Encourage employees to do the desirable things they will do anyway.
G.  Judge your supervision by the results it secures.

VII.   Principle of Science
Successful supervision is scientific, objective, and experimental.  It is based on facts, not on prejudices.
   A.   Be cumulative in results.
   B.   Never divorce your suggestions from the goals of training.
   C.   Don't be impatient of results.
   D.   Keep all matters on a professional, not a personal, level.
   E.   Do not be concerned exclusively with immediate problems and activities.
   F.   Use objective means of determining achievement and rating where possible.

VIII.  Principle of Cooperation
Supervision is a cooperative enterprise between supervisor and employee.
   A.   Begin with conditions as they are.
   B.   Ask opinions of all involved when formulating policies.
   C.   Organization is as good as its weakest link.
   D.   Let employees help to determine policies and department programs.
   E.   Be approachable and accessible—physically and mentally.
   F.   Develop pleasant social relationships.

## WHAT IS ADMINISTRATION

Administration is concerned with providing the environment, the material facilities, and the operational procedures that will promote the maximum growth and development of supervisors and employees.  (Organization is an aspect and a concomitant of administration.)

There is no sharp line of demarcation between supervision and administration; these functions are intimately interrelated and, often, overlapping.  They are complementary activities.

I.   Practices Commonly Classed as "Supervisory"
   A.   Conducting employees' conferences
   B.   Visiting sections, units, offices, divisions, departments
   C.   Arranging for demonstrations
   D.   Examining plans
   E.   Suggesting professional reading
   F.   Interpreting bulletins
   G.   Recommending in-service training courses
   H.   Encouraging experimentation
   I.   Appraising employee morale
   J.   Providing for intervisitation

II.   Practices Commonly Classified as "Administrative"
   A.   Management of the office
   B.   Arrangement of schedules for extra duties
   C.   Assignment of rooms or areas
   D.   Distribution of supplies
   E.   Keeping records and reports
   F.   Care of audio-visual materials
   G.   Keeping inventory records
   H.   Checking record cards and books

I.   Programming special activities
J.   Checking on the attendance and punctuality of employees

III.  Practices Commonly Classified as Both "Supervisory" and "Administrative"
A.   Program construction
B.   Testing or evaluating outcomes
C.   Personnel accounting
D.   Ordering instructional materials

## RESPONSIBILITIES OF THE SUPERVISOR

A person employed in a supervisory capacity must constantly be able to improve his own efficiency and ability. He represent the employer to the employees and only continuous self-examination can make him a capable supervisor.

Leadership and training are the supervisor's responsibility. An efficient working unit is one in which the employees work with the supervisor. It is his job to bring out the best in his employees. He must always be relaxed, courteous, and calm in his association with his employees. Their feelings are important, and a harsh attitude does not develop the most efficient employees.

## COMPETENCES OF THE SUPERVISOR

I.    Complete knowledge of the duties and responsibilities of his position.
II.   To be able to organize a job, plan ahead, and carry through.
III.  To have self-confidence and initiative.
IV.   To be able to handle the unexpected situation and make quick decisions.
V.    To be able to properly train subordinates in the positions they are best suited for.
VI.   To be able to keep good human relations among his subordinates.
VII.  To be able to keep good human relations between his subordinates and himself and to earn their respect and trust.

## THE PROFESSIONAL SUPERVISOR-EMPLOYEE RELATIONSHIP

There are two kinds of efficiency: one kind is only apparent and is produced in organizations through the exercise of mere discipline; this is but a simulation of the second, or true, efficiency which springs from spontaneous cooperation. If you are a manager, no matter how great or small your responsibility, it is your job, in the final analysis, to create and develop this involuntary cooperation among the people whom you supervise. For, no matter how powerful a combination of money, machines, and materials a company may have, this is a dead and sterile thing without a team of willing, thinking, and articulate people to guide it.

The following 21 points are presented as indicative of the exemplary basic relationship that should exist between supervisor and employee:

1.   Each person wants to be liked and respected by his fellow employee and wants to be treated with consideration and respect by his superior.
2.   The most competent employee will make an error. However, in a unit where good relations exist between the supervisor and his employees, tenseness and fear do not exist. Thus, errors are not hidden or covered up, and the efficiency of a unit is not impaired.

3. Subordinates resent rules, regulations, or orders that are unreasonable or unexplained.
4. Subordinates are quick to resent unfairness, harshness, injustices, and favoritism.
5. An employee will accept responsibility if he knows that he will be complimented for a job well done, and not too harshly chastised for failure; that his supervisor will check the cause of the failure, and, if it was the supervisor's fault, he will assume the blame therefore. If it was the employee's fault, his supervisor will explain the correct method or means of handling the responsibility.
6. An employee wants to receive credit for a suggestion he has made, that is used. If a suggestion cannot be used, the employee is entitled to an explanation. The supervisor should not say "no" and close the subject.
7. Fear and worry slow up a worker's ability. Poor working environment can impair his physical and mental health. A good supervisor avoids forceful methods, threats, and arguments to get a job done.
8. A forceful supervisor is able to train his employees individually and as a team, and is able to motivate them in the proper channels.
9. A mature supervisor is able to properly evaluate his subordinates and to keep them happy and satisfied.
10. A sensitive supervisor will never patronize his subordinates.
11. A worthy supervisor will respect his employees' confidences.
12. Definite and clear-cut responsibilities should be assigned to each executive.
13. Responsibility should always be coupled with corresponding authority.
14. No change should be made in the scope or responsibilities of a position without a definite understanding to that effect on the part of all persons concerned.
15. No executive or employee, occupying a single position in the organization, should be subject to definite orders from more than one source.
16. Orders should never be given to subordinates over the head of a responsible executive. Rather than do this, the officer in question should be supplanted.
17. Criticisms of subordinates should, whoever possible, be made privately, and in no case should a subordinate be criticized in the presence of executives or employees of equal or lower rank.
18. No dispute or difference between executives or employees as to authority or responsibilities should be considered too trivial for prompt and careful adjudication.
19. Promotions, wage changes, and disciplinary action should always be approved by the executive immediately superior to the one directly responsible.
20. No executive or employee should ever be required, or expected, to be at the same time an assistant to, and critic of, another.
21. Any executive whose work is subject to regular inspection should, wherever practicable, be given the assistance and facilities necessary to enable him to maintain an independent check of the quality of his work.

## MINI-TEXT IN SUPERVISION, ADMINISTRATION, MANAGEMENT, AND ORGANIZATION

I. Brief Highlights

Listed concisely and sequentially are major headings and important data in the field for quick recall and review.

A. Levels of Management
Any organization of some size has several levels of management. In terms of a ladder, the levels are:

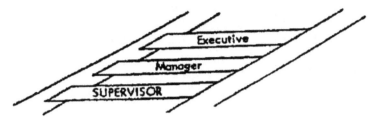

The first level is very important because it is the beginning point of management leadership.

B. What the Supervisor Must Learn
A supervisor must learn to:
1. Deal with people and their differences
2. Get the job done through people
3. Recognize the problems when they exist
4. Overcome obstacles to good performance
5. Evaluate the performance of people
6. Check his own performance in terms of accomplishment

C. A Definition of Supervisor
The term supervisor means any individual having authority, in the interests of the employer, to hire, transfer, suspend, lay-off, recall, promote, discharge, assign, reward, or discipline other employees or responsibility to direct them, or to adjust their grievances, or effectively to recommend such action, if, in connection with the foregoing, exercise of such authority is not of a merely routine or clerical nature but requires the use of independent judgment.

D. Elements of the Team Concept
What is involved in teamwork? The component parts are:
1. Members
2. A leader
3. Goals
4. Plans
5. Cooperation
6. Spirit

E. Principles of Organization
1. A team member must know what his job is.
2. Be sure that the nature and scope of a job are understood.
3. Authority and responsibility should be carefully spelled out.
4. A supervisor should be permitted to make the maximum number of decisions affecting his employees.
5. Employees should report to only one supervisor.
6. A supervisor should direct only as many employees as he can handle effectively.
7. An organization plan should be flexible.

8.    Inspection and performance of work should be separate.
9.    Organizational problems should receive immediate attention.
10.   Assign work in line with ability and experience.

F.    The Four Important Parts of Every Job
    1.    Inherent in every job is the *accountability* for results.
    2.    A second set of factors in every job is *responsibilities.*
    3.    Along with duties and responsibilities one must have the *authority* to act within certain limits without obtaining permission to proceed.
    4.    No job exists in a vacuum.  The supervisor is surrounded by key *relationships.*

G.    Principles of Delegation
    Where work is delegated for the first time, the supervisor should think in terms of these questions:
    1.    Who is best qualified to do this?
    2.    Can an employee improve his abilities by doing this?
    3.    How long should an employee spend on this?
    4.    Are there any special problems for which he will need guidance?
    5.    How broad a delegation can I make?

H.    Principles of Effective Communications
    1.    Determine the media.
    2.    To whom directed?
    3.    Identification and source authority.
    4.    Is communication understood?

I.    Principles of Work Improvement
    1.    Most people usually do only the work which is assigned to them.
    2.    Workers are likely to fit assigned work into the time available to perform it.
    3.    A good workload usually stimulates output.
    4.    People usually do their best work when they know that results will be reviewed or inspected.
    5.    Employees usually feel that someone else is responsible for conditions of work, workplace layout, job methods, type of tools/equipment, and other such factors.
    6.    Employees are usually defensive about their job security.
    7.    Employees have natural resistance to change.
    8.    Employees can support or destroy a supervisor.
    9.    A supervisor usually earns the respect of his people through his personal example of diligence and efficiency.

J.    Areas of Job Improvement
    The areas of job improvement are quite numerous, but the most common ones which a supervisor can identify and utilize are:
    1.    Departmental layout
    2.    Flow of work
    3.    Workplace layout
    4.    Utilization of manpower
    5.    Work methods
    6.    Materials handling

7.  Utilization
8.  Motion economy

K.  Seven Key Points in Making Improvements
    1.  Select the job to be improved
    2.  Study how it is being done now
    3.  Question the present method
    4.  Determine actions to be taken
    5.  Chart proposed method
    6.  Get approval and apply
    7.  Solicit worker participation

I.  Corrective Techniques of Job Improvement
Specific Problems
    1.  Size of workload
    2.  Inability to meet schedules
    3.  Strain and fatigue
    4.  Improper use of men and skills
    5.  Waste, poor quality, unsafe conditions
    6.  Bottleneck conditions that hinder output
    7.  Poor utilization of equipment and machine
    8.  Efficiency and productivity of labor

General Improvement
    1.  Departmental layout
    2.  Flow of work
    3.  Work plan layout
    4.  Utilization of manpower
    5.  Work methods
    6.  Materials handling
    7.  Utilization of equipment
    8.  Motion economy

Corrective Techniques
    1.  Study with scale model
    2.  Flow chart study
    3.  Motion analysis
    4.  Comparison of units produced to standard allowance
    5.  Methods analysis
    6.  Flow chart and equipment study
    7.  Down time vs. running time
    8.  Motion analysis

M.  A Planning Checklist
    1.  Objectives
    2.  Controls
    3.  Delegations
    4.  Communications
    5.  Resources
    6.  Manpower

7. Equipment
8. Supplies and materials
9. Utilization of time
10. Safety
11. Money
12. Work
13. Timing of improvements

N. Five Characteristics of Good Directions
In order to get results, directions must be:
1. Possible of accomplishment
2. Agreeable with worker interests
3. Related to mission
4. Planned and complete
5. Unmistakably clear

O. Types of Directions
1. Demands or direct orders
2. Requests
3. Suggestion or implication
4. volunteering

P. Controls
A typical listing of the overall areas in which the supervisor should establish controls might be:
1. Manpower
2. Materials
3. Quality of work
4. Quantity of work
5. Time
6. Space
7. Money
8. Methods

Q. Orienting the New Employee
1. Prepare for him
2. Welcome the new employee
3. Orientation for the job
4. Follow-up

R. Checklist for Orienting New Employees     Yes   No
1. Do you appreciate the feelings of new employees when they first report for work? ___ ___
2. Are you aware of the fact that the new employee must make a big adjustment to his job? ___ ___
3. Have you given him good reasons for liking the job and the organization? ___ ___
4. Have you prepared for his first day on the job? ___ ___
5. Did you welcome him cordially and make him feel needed? ___ ___

|  | Yes | No |
|---|---|---|

6.   Did you establish rapport with him so that he feels free to talk and discuss matters with you?   ____   ____

7.   Did you explain his job to him and his relationship to you?   ____   ____

8.   Does he know that his work will be evaluated periodically on a basis that is fair and objective?   ____   ____

9.   Did you introduce him to his fellow workers in such a way that they are likely to accept him?   ____   ____

10.   Does he know what employee benefits he will receive?   ____   ____

11.   Does he understand the importance of being on the job and what to do if he must leave his duty station?   ____   ____

12.   Has he been impressed with the importance of accident prevention and safe practice?   ____   ____

13.   Does he generally know his way around the department?   ____   ____

14.   Is he under the guidance of a sponsor who will teach the right way of doing things?   ____   ____

15.   Do you plan to follow-up so that he will continue to adjust successfully to his job?   ____   ____

S.   Principles of Learning
   1.   Motivation
   2.   Demonstration or explanation
   3.   Practice

T.   Causes of Poor Performance
   1.   Improper training for job
   2.   Wrong tools
   3.   Inadequate directions
   4.   Lack of supervisory follow-up
   5.   Poor communications
   6.   Lack of standards of performance
   7.   Wrong work habits
   8.   Low morale
   9.   Other

U.   Four Major Steps in On-The-Job Instruction
   1.   Prepare the worker
   2.   Present the operation
   3.   Tryout performance
   4.   Follow-up

V.   Employees Want Five Things
   1.   Security
   2.   Opportunity
   3.   Recognition
   4.   Inclusion
   5.   Expression

W. Some Don'ts in Regard to Praise
1. Don't praise a person for something he hasn't done.
2. Don't praise a person unless you can be sincere.
3. Don't be sparing in praise just because your superior withholds it from you.
4. Don't let too much time elapse between good performance and recognition of it

X. How to Gain Your Workers' Confidence
Methods of developing confidence include such things as:
1. Knowing the interests, habits, hobbies of employees
2. Admitting your own inadequacies
3. Sharing and telling of confidence in others
4. Supporting people when they are in trouble
5. Delegating matters that can be well handled
6. Being frank and straightforward about problems and working conditions
7. Encouraging others to bring their problems to you
8. Taking action on problems which impede worker progress

Y. Sources of Employee Problems
On-the-job causes might be such things as:
1. A feeling that favoritism is exercised in assignments
2. Assignment of overtime
3. An undue amount of supervision
4. Changing methods or systems
5. Stealing of ideas or trade secrets
6. Lack of interest in job
7. Threat of reduction in force
8. Ignorance or lack of communications
9. Poor equipment
10. Lack of knowing how supervisor feels toward employee
11. Shift assignments

Off-the-job problems might have to do with:
1. Health
2. Finances
3. Housing
4. Family

Z. The Supervisor's Key to Discipline
There are several key points about discipline which the supervisor should keep in mind:
1. Job discipline is one of the disciplines of life and is directed by the supervisor.
2. It is more important to correct an employee fault than to fix blame for it.
3. Employee performance is affected by problems both on the job and off.
4. Sudden or abrupt changes in behavior can be indications of important employee problems.
5. Problems should be dealt with as soon as possible after they are identified.
6. The attitude of the supervisor may have more to do with solving problems than the techniques of problem solving.
7. Correction of employee behavior should be resorted to only after the supervisor is sure that training or counseling will not be helpful.

8. Be sure to document your disciplinary actions.
9. Make sure that you are disciplining on the basis of facts rather than personal feelings.
10. Take each disciplinary step in order, being careful not to make snap judgments, or decisions based on impatience.

AA. Five Important Processes of Management
1. Planning
2. Organizing
3. Scheduling
4. Controlling
5. Motivating

BB. When the Supervisor Fails to Plan
1. Supervisor creates impression of not knowing his job
2. May lead to excessive overtime
3. Job runs itself—supervisor lacks control
4. Deadlines and appointments missed
5. Parts of the work go undone
6. Work interrupted by emergencies
7. Sets a bad example
8. Uneven workload creates peaks and valleys
9. Too much time on minor details at expense of more important tasks

CC. Fourteen General Principles of Management
1. Division of work
2. Authority and responsibility
3. Discipline
4. Unity of command
5. Unity of direction
6. Subordination of individual interest to general interest
7. Remuneration of personnel
8. Centralization
9. Scalar chain
10. Order
11. Equity
12. Stability of tenure of personnel
13. Initiative
14. Esprit de corps

DD. Change

Bringing about change is perhaps attempted more often, and yet less well understood, than anything else the supervisor does. How do people generally react to change? (People tend to resist change that is imposed upon them by other individuals or circumstances.

Change is characteristic of every situation. It is a part of every real endeavor where the efforts of people are concerned.

1. Why do people resist change?
   People may resist change because of:
   a. Fear of the unknown
   b. Implied criticism
   c. Unpleasant experiences in the past
   d. Fear of loss of status
   e. Threat to the ego
   f. Fear of loss of economic stability

2. How can we best overcome the resistance to change?
   In initiating change, take these steps:
   a. Get ready to sell
   b. Identify sources of help
   c. Anticipate objections
   d. Sell benefits
   e. Listen in depth
   f. Follow up

II. Brief Topical Summaries

A. Who/What is the Supervisor?
   1. The supervisor is often called the "highest level employee and the lowest level manager."
   2. A supervisor is a member of both management and the work group. He acts as a bridge between the two.
   3. Most problems in supervision are in the area of human relations, or people problems.
   4. Employees expect: Respect, opportunity to learn and to advance, and a sense of belonging, and so forth.
   5. Supervisors are responsible for directing people and organizing work. Planning is of paramount importance.
   6. A position description is a set of duties and responsibilities inherent to a given position.
   7. It is important to keep the position description up-to-date and to provide each employee with his own copy.

B. The Sociology of Work
   1. People are alike in many ways; however, each individual is unique.
   2. The supervisor is challenged in getting to know employee differences. Acquiring skills in evaluating individuals is an asset.
   3. Maintaining meaningful working relationships in the organization is of great importance.
   4. The supervisor has an obligation to help individuals to develop to their fullest potential.
   5. Job rotation on a planned basis helps to build versatility and to maintain interest and enthusiasm in work groups.
   6. Cross training (job rotation) provides backup skills.

7. The supervisor can help reduce tension by maintaining a sense of humor, providing guidance to employees, and by making reasonable and timely decisions. Employees respond favorably to working under reasonably predictable circumstances.
8. Change is characteristic of all managerial behavior. The supervisor must adjust to changes in procedures, new methods, technological changes, and to a number of new and sometimes challenging situations.
9. To overcome the natural tendency for people to resist change, the supervisor should become more skillful in initiating change.

C. Principles and Practices of Supervision
1. Employees should be required to answer to only one superior.
2. A supervisor can effectively direct only a limited number of employees, depending upon the complexity, variety, and proximity of the jobs involved.
3. The organizational chart presents the organization in graphic form. It reflects lines of authority and responsibility as well as interrelationships of units within the organization.
4. Distribution of work can be improved through an analysis using the "Work Distribution Chart."
5. The "Work Distribution Chart" reflects the division of work within a unit in understandable form.
6. When related tasks are given to an employee, he has a better chance of increasing his skills through training.
7. The individual who is given the responsibility for tasks must also be given the appropriate authority to insure adequate results.
8. The supervisor should delegate repetitive, routine work. Preparation of recurring reports, maintaining leave and attendance records are some examples.
9. Good discipline is essential to good task performance. Discipline is reflected in the actions of employees on the job in the absence of supervision.
10. Disciplinary action may have to be taken when the positive aspects of discipline have failed. Reprimand, warning, and suspension are examples of disciplinary action.
11. If a situation calls for a reprimand, be sure it is deserved and remember it is to be done in private.

D. Dynamic Leadership
1. A style is a personal method or manner of exerting influence.
2. Authoritarian leaders often see themselves as the source of power and authority.
3. The democratic leader often perceives the group as the source of authority and power.
4. Supervisors tend to do better when using the pattern of leadership that is most natural for them.
5. Social scientists suggest that the effective supervisor use the leadership style that best fits the problem or circumstances involved.
6. All four styles—telling, selling, consulting, joining—have their place. Using one does not preclude using the other at another time.

7. The theory X point of view assumes that the average person dislikes work, will avoid it whenever possible, and must be coerced to achieve organizational objectives.

8. The theory Y point of view assumes that the average person considers work to be a natural as play, and, when the individual is committed, he requires little supervision or direction to accomplish desired objectives.

9. The leader's basic assumptions concerning human behavior and human nature affect his actions, decisions, and other managerial practices.

10. Dissatisfaction among employees is often present, but difficult to isolate. The supervisor should seek to weaken dissatisfaction by keeping promises, being sincere and considerate, keeping employees informed, and so forth.

11. Constructive suggestions should be encouraged during the natural progress of the work.

E. Processes for Solving Problems

1. People find their daily tasks more meaningful and satisfying when they can improve them.

2. The causes of problems, or the key factors, are often hidden in the background. Ability to solve problems often involves the ability to isolate them from their backgrounds. There is some substance to the cliché that some persons "can't see the forest for the trees."

3. New procedures are often developed from old ones. Problems should be broken down into manageable parts. New ideas can be adapted from old one.

4. People think differently in problem-solving situations. Using a logical, patterned approach is often useful. One approach found to be useful includes these steps:
   a. Define the problem
   b. Establish objectives
   c. Get the facts
   d. Weigh and decide
   e. Take action
   f. Evaluate action

F. Training for Results

1. Participants respond best when they feel training is important to them.

2. The supervisor has responsibility for the training and development of those who report to him.

3. When training is delegated to others, great care must be exercised to insure the trainer has knowledge, aptitude, and interest for his work as a trainer.

4. Training (learning) of some type goes on continually. The most successful supervisor makes certain the learning contributes in a productive manner to operational goals.

5. New employees are particularly susceptible to training. Older employees facing new job situations require specific training, as well as having need for development and growth opportunities.

6. Training needs require continuous monitoring.

7. The training officer of an agency is a professional with a responsibility to assist supervisors in solving training problems.

8. Many of the self-development steps important to the supervisor's own growth are equally important to the development of peers and subordinates. Knowledge of these is important when the supervisor consults with others on development and growth opportunities.

G. Health, Safety, and Accident Prevention
1. Management-minded supervisors take appropriate measures to assist employees in maintaining health and in assuring safe practices in the work environment.
2. Effective safety training and practices help to avoid injury and accidents.
3. Safety should be a management goal. All infractions of safety which are observed should be corrected without exception.
4. Employees' safety attitude, training and instruction, provision of safe tools and equipment, supervision, and leadership are considered highly important factors which contribute to safety and which can be influenced directly by supervisors.
5. When accidents do occur, they should be investigated promptly for very important reasons, including the fact that information which is gained can be used to prevent accidents in the future.

H. Equal Employment Opportunity
1. The supervisor should endeavor to treat all employees fairly, without regard to religion, race, sex, or national origin.
2. Groups tend to reflect the attitude of the leader. Prejudice can be detected even in very subtle form. Supervisors must strive to create a feeling of mutual respect and confidence in every employee.
3. Complete utilization of all human resources is a national goal. Equitable consideration should be accorded women in the work force, minority-group members, the physically and mentally handicapped, and the older employee. The important question is: "Who can do the job?"
4. Training opportunities, recognition for performance, overtime assignments, promotional opportunities, and all other personnel actions are to be handled on an equitable basis.

I. Improving Communications
1. Communications is achieving understanding between the sender and the receiver of a message. It also means sharing information—the creation of understanding.
2. Communication is basic to all human activity. Words are means of conveying meanings; however, real meanings are in people.
3. There are very practical differences in the effectiveness of one-way, impersonal, and two-way communications. Words spoken face-to-face are better understood. Telephone conversations are effective, but lack the rapport of person-to-person exchanges. The whole person communicates.
4. Cooperation and communication in an organization go hand in hand. When there is a mutual respect between people, spelling out rules and procedures for communicating is unnecessary.
5. There are several barriers to effective communications. These include failure to listen with respect and understanding, lack of skill in feedback, and misinterpreting the meanings of words used by the speaker. It is also common

practice to listen to what we want to hear, and tune out things we do not want to hear.

6. Communication is management's chief problem. The supervisor should accept the challenge to communicate more effectively and to improve interagency and intra-agency communications.
7. The supervisor may often plan for and conduct meetings. The planning phase is critical and may determine the success or the failure of a meeting.
8. Speaking before groups usually requires extra effort. Stage fright may never disappear completely, but it can be controlled.

J. Self-Development
1. Every employee is responsible for his own self-development.
2. Toastmaster and toastmistress clubs offer opportunities to improve skills in oral communications.
3. Planning for one's own self-development is of vital importance. Supervisors know their own strengths and limitations better than anyone else.
4. Many opportunities are open to aid the supervisor in his developmental efforts, including job assignments; training opportunities, both governmental and non-governmental—to include universities and professional conferences and seminars.
5. Programmed instruction offers a means of studying at one's own rate.
6. Where difficulties may arise from a supervisor's being away from his work for training, he may participate in televised home study or correspondence courses to meet his self-development needs.

K. Teaching and Training
1. The Teaching Process
Teaching is encouraging and guiding the learning activities of students toward established goals. In most cases this process consists of five steps: preparation, presentation, summarization, evaluation, and application.

 a. Preparation
 Preparation is two-fold in nature; that of the supervisor and the employee. Preparation by the supervisor is absolutely essential to success. He must know what, when, where, how, and whom he will teach. Some of the factors that should be considered are:
 1) The objectives
 2) The materials needed
 3) The methods to be used
 4) Employee participation
 5) Employee interest
 6) Training aids
 7) Evaluation
 8) Summarization

 Employee preparation consists in preparing the employee to receive the material. Probably the most important single factor in the preparation of the employee is arousing and maintaining his interest. He must know the objectives of the training, why he is there, how the material can be used, and its importance to him.

b. Presentation
   In presentation, have a carefully designed plan and follow it. The plan should be accurate and complete, yet flexible enough to meet situations as they arise. The method of presentation will be determined by the particular situation and objectives.

c. Summary
   A summary should be made at the end of every training unit and program. In addition, there may be internal summaries depending on the nature of the material being taught. The important thing is that the trainee must always be able to understand how each part of the new material relates to the whole.

d. Application
   The supervisor must arrange work so the employee will be given a chance to apply new knowledge or skills while the material is still clear in his mind and interest is high. The trainee does not really know whether he has learned the material until he has been given a chance to apply it. If the material is not applied, it loses most of its value.

e. Evaluation
   The purpose of all training is to promote learning. To determine whether the training has been a success or failure, the supervisor must evaluate this learning.
   In the broadest sense, evaluation includes all the devices, methods, skills, and techniques used by the supervisor to keep himself and the employees informed as to their progress toward the objectives they are pursuing. The extent to which the employee has mastered the knowledge, skills, and abilities, or changed his attitudes, as determined by the program objectives, is the extent to which instruction has succeeded or failed.
   Evaluation should not be confined to the end of the lesson, day, or program but should be used continuously. We shall note later the way this relates to the rest of the teaching process.

2. Teaching Methods
   A teaching method is a pattern of identifiable student and instructor activity used in presenting training material.
   All supervisors are faced with the problem of deciding which method should be used at a given time.

   a. Lecture
      The lecture is direct oral presentation of material by the supervisor. The present trend is to place less emphasis on the trainer's activity and more on that of the trainee.

   b. Discussion
      Teaching by discussion or conference involves using questions and other techniques to arouse interest and focus attention upon certain areas, and by doing so creating a learning situation. This can be one of the most

valuable methods because it gives the employees an opportunity to express their ideas and pool their knowledge.

c.  Demonstration
The demonstration is used to teach how something works or how to do something.  It can be used to show a principle or what the results of a series of actions will be.  A well-staged demonstration is particularly effective because it shows proper methods of performance in a realistic manner.

d.  Performance
Performance is one of the most fundamental of all learning techniques or teaching methods.  The trainee may be able to tell how a specific operation should be performed but he cannot be sure he knows how to perform the operation until he has done so.
As with all methods, there are certain advantages and disadvantages to each method.

e.  Which Method to Use
Moreover, there are other methods and techniques of teaching.  It is difficult to use any method without other methods entering into it.  In any learning situation, a combination of methods is usually more effective than any one method alone.

Finally, evaluation must be integrated into the other aspects of the teaching-learning process.

It must be used in the motivation of the trainees; it must be used to assist in developing understanding during the training; and it must be related to employee application of the results of training.

This is distinctly the role of the supervisor.

———

# BASIC FUNDAMENTALS OF BOOKKEEPING

## CONTENTS

# BASIC FUNDAMENTALS OF BOOKKEEPING

## I. INTRODUCTION

Why keep records? If you are a typical small-business man, your answer to this question is probably, "Because the Government requires it!" And if the question comes in the middle of a busy day, you may add a few heartfelt words about the amount of time you have to spend on records--just for the Government.

Is it "just for the Government," though? True, regulations of various governmental agencies have greatly increased the record-keeping requirements of business. But this may be a good thing for the small-business man, overburdened though he is.

Many small-business managers don't recognize their bookkeeping records for what they can really do. Their attitudes concerning these records are typified by one businessman who said, "Records only tell you what you have done in the past. It's too late to do anything about the past; I need to know what is going to happen in the future. "However, the past can tell us much about what may happen in the future; and, certainly we can profit in the future from knowledge of our past mistakes.

These same managers may recognize that records are necessary in filing their tax returns, or that a banker requires financial information before he will lend money, but often their appreciation of their bookkeeping systems ends at this point. However, there are many ways in which the use of such information can help an owner manage his business more easily and profitably.

The small-businessman is confronted with an endless array of problems and decisions every day. Sound decisions require an informed manager; and many management problems can be solved with the aid of the right bookkeeping information.

## II. REQUIREMENTS OF A GOOD RECORD SYSTEM

Of course, to get information that is really valuable to you--to get the right information--requires a good bookkeeping system. What are the characteristics of a good system? You want one that is simple and easy to understand, reliable, accurate, consistent, and one that will get the information to you promptly.

A simple, well-organized system of records, regularly kept up, can actually be a timesaver--by bringing order out of disorder. Furthermore, competition is very strong in today's business areas. A businessman needs to know almost on a day-to-day basis where his business stands profit wise, which lines of merchandise or services are the most or the least profitable, what his working-capital needs are, and many other details. He can get this information with reasonable certainty only if he has a good recordkeeping system—one that gives him all the information he needs.

In setting up a recordkeeping system that is tailored to your business, you will probably need the professional help of a competent accountant. And you may want to retain the services of an accountant or bookkeeper to maintain these records. But it is your job to learn to interpret this information and to use it effectively.

One of the reasons that many managers have misgivings about keeping records is that they don't understand them or know how they can be used. The owner or manager of a small business may be an expert in his line of business; however, he generally does not have a background in keeping records. So he is usually confused. What we will try to do in this discussion is to highlight the "why and what of bookkeeping." In so-doing, we aim to eliminate that confusion.

# III. IMPORTANT BOOKKEEPING RECORDS

Today's managers should be familiar with the following bookkeeping records:

- Journal
- Ledgers
- Balance sheet
- Income statement
- Funds flow statement

We will discuss each of them in turn. In addition, a brief discussion of other supporting records will be made.

## A. Bookkeeping Books

The journal, which accountants call "the book of original entry," is a chronological record of all business transactions engaged in by the firm. It is simply a financial diary. The ledgers, or "books of account," are more specialized records used to classify the journal entries according to like elements. For example, there would be a separate ledger account for cash entries, another for all sales, and still others for items such as accounts receivable, inventory, and loans. All transactions are first entered in the journal, and then posted in the appropriate ledger. The journal and ledgers are of minor importance to the manager in making decisions, but they play a vital role for the accountant or bookkeeper because the more important accounting statements such as the balance sheet and the income statement are derived from the journal and ledger entries.

## B. Financial Reports

The two principal financial reports in most businesses are the balance sheet and the income statement. Up to about 25 or 30 years ago, the balance sheet was generally considered to be the most important financial statement. Until that time, it was generally used only as a basis for the extension of credit and bank loans, and very little thought was given to the information it offered that might be important in „the operation and management of the business. Starting about 30 years ago, emphasis has gradually shifted to the income statement. Today the balance sheet and income statements are of equal importance, both to the accountant in financial reporting and to the manager faced with a multitude of administrative problems.

Essentially, the balance sheet shows what a business has, what it owes, and the investment of the owners in the business. It can be likened to a snapshot, showing the financial condition of the business *at a certain point in time*. The income statement, on the other hand, is a summary of business operations for a certain period--usually between two balance sheet dates. The income statement can be compared to a moving picture; it indicates the activity of a business *over a certain period of time*. In very general terms, the balance sheet tells you where you are, and the income statement tells you how you got there since the last time you had a balance sheet prepared.

Both the balance sheet and income statement can be long and complicated documents. Both accountants and management need some device that can highlight the critical financial information contained in these complex documents. Certain standard ratios or relationships between items on the financial statements have been developed that allow the interested parties to quickly determine important characteristics of the firm's activities. There are many relationships that might be important in a specific business that would not be as significant in another.

Other devices of the bookkeeper, such as funds flow statements, daily summaries of sales and cash receipts, the checkbook, account receivable records, property depreciation records, and insurance scheduling have also been found useful to management.

## C. The Balance Sheet

As stated earlier, the balance sheet represents what a business has, what it owes, and the investment of the owners. The things of value that the business has or owns are called *assets*. The claims of creditors against these assets are called liabilities. The value of the assets over and above the *liabilities* can be justifiably called the owner's claim. This amount is usually called the owner's equity (or net worth).

This brings us to the *dual-aspect concept* of bookkeeping. The balance sheet is set up to portray two aspects of each entry or event recorded on it. For each thing of value, or asset, there is a claim against that asset. The recognition of this concept leads to the balance sheet formula: ASSETS = LIABILITIES + OWNER'S EQUITY. Let's take an example to clarify this concept. Suppose Joe Smith decides to start a business. He has $2,000 cash in the bank. He got this sum by investing $1,000 of his own money and by borrowing $1,000 from the bank. If he were to draw up a balance sheet at this time, he would have assets of $2 000 cash balanced against a liability claim of $1,000 and an owner's claim of $1,000. Using the balance sheet formula: $2,000 = $1,000 + $1,000. This formula means there will always be a balance between assets and claims against them. The balance sheet *always* balances unless there has been a clerical error.

The balance sheet is usually, constructed in a two-column format. The assets appear in the left hand column and the claims against the assets (the liabilities and owner's equity) are in the right hand column. Other formats are sometimes used; but, in any case, the balance sheet is-an itemized or detailed account of the basic formula: as sets = liabilities + owner's equity.

## 1. Assets

I have been speaking of assets belonging to the business. Of course, the business does not legally own anything unless it is organized as a corporation. But regardless of whether the business is organized as a proprietorship, a partnership, or a corporation, all business book-keeping should be reckoned and accounted apart from the accounting of the personal funds and assets of, its owners.

Assets are typically classified into three categories:

- Current assets
- Fixed assets
- Other assets

## a. Current Assets

For bookkeeping purposes, the term "current assets" is used to designate cash and other assets which can be converted to cash during the normal operating cycle of the business (usually one year). The distinction between current assets and noncurrent assets is important since lenders and others pay much attention to the total amount of current assets. The size of current assets has a significant relationship to the stability of the business because it represents, to some degree, the amount of cash that might be raised quickly to meet current obligations. Here are some of the major current asset items.

**Cash** consists of funds that are immediately available to use without restrictions. These funds are usually in the form of checking-account deposits in banks, cash-register money, and petty cash. Cash should be large enough to meet obligations that are immediately due.

**Accounts, receivable** are Arricnint8 'Owed to the company by its customers as a result of sales. Essentially, these accounts are the result of granting credit to customers. They may take the form of charge accounts where no interest or service charge is made, or they may be of an interest-bearing nature. In either case they are a drain on working capital. The more that is outstanding on accounts receivable, the less money that is available to meet current needs. The trick with accounts receivable is to keep them small enough so as not to endanger working capital, but large enough to keep from losing sales to credit-minded customers.

**Inventory** is defined as those items which are held for sale in the ordinary course of business, or which are to be consumed in the production of goods and services that are to be sold. Since accountants are conservative by nature, they include in inventory only items that are salable, and these items are valued at cost or market value, whichever is lower? Control of inventory and inventory expenses is one of management's most important jobs-particularly for retailers-- and good bookkeeping records in this area are particularly useful.

**Prepaid expenses** represent assets, paid for in advance, but whose usefulness will usually expire in a short time. A good example of this is prepaid insurance. A business pays for insurance protection in advance--usually three to five years in advance. The right to this protection is a thing of value--an asset--and the unused portion can be refunded or converted to cash.

## b. Fixed Assets

"Fixed assets" are items owned by the business that have relatively long life. These assets are used in the production or sale of other goods and services. If they were held for resale, they would be classified as inventory, even though they might be long-lived assets.

Normally these assets are composed of land, buildings, and equipment. Some companies lump their fixed assets into one entry on their balance sheets, but you gain more information and can exercise more control over these assets if they are listed separately on the balance sheet. You may even want to list various types of equipment separately.

There is one other aspect of fixed-asset bookkeeping that we should discuss--and this is depreciation. Generally fixed assets-with the exception of land-depreciate, or decrease in value with the passing of time. That is, a building or piece of equipment that is five years old is not worth as much as it was when it was new. For a balance sheet to show the true value of these assets, it must reflect this loss in value. For both tax and other accounting purposes, the businessman is allowed to deduct this loss in value each year over the useful life of the assets, until, over a period of time, he has deducted the total cost of the asset. There are several accepted ways to calculate how much of an asset's value can be deducted for depreciation in a given year. Depreciation is allowed as an expense item on the income statement, and we will discuss this fact later.

### c. Other Assets

"Other assets" is a miscellaneous category. It accounts for any investments of the firm in securities, such as stock in other private companies or government bonds. It also includes intangible assets such as goodwill, patents, and franchise costs. Items in the "other-assets" category have a longer life than current-asset items.

## 2. Liabilities

"Liabilities" are the amounts of money owed by the business to people other than the owners. They are claims against the company's total assets, although they are not claims against any specific asset, except in the cases of some mortgages and equipment liens. Essentially, liabilities are divided into two classes:

Current liabilities

Long-term Liabilities

### a. Current Liabilities

The term "current liabilities" is used to describe those claims of outsiders on the business that will fall, due within one year. Here are some of the more important current-liabilities entries on the balance sheet:

**Accounts payable** represent the amounts owed to vendors, wholesalers, and other suppliers from whom the business has bought items on account. This includes any items of inventory, supply, or capital equipment which have been purchased on credit and for which payment is expected in less than one year. For example, a retail butcher purchased 500 pounds of meat for $250, a quantity of fish that cost $50, and a new air-conditioning unit for his store for $450. He bought all of these items on 60-day terms. His accounts payable were increased by $750. Of course, at the same time his inventory increased by $300 and his fixed assets rose by $450. If he had paid cash for these items, his accounts payable would not have been affected, but his cash account would have decreased by $750, thus keeping the accounting equation in balance.

**Short-term loans**, which are sometimes called notes payable, are loans from individuals, banks, or other lending institutions which fall due within a year. Also included in this category is the portion of any long-term debt that will come due within a year.

**Accrued expenses** are obligations which the company has incurred, but for 'which there has been no formal bill or invoice as yet. An example of this is accrued taxes. The owner knows the business has the obligation to pay taxes; and they are accruing or accumulating each day. The fact that the taxes do not have to be paid until a later date does not diminish the obligation. Another example of accrued expenses is wages. Although wages are paid weekly or monthly, they are being earned hourly or daily and constitute a valid claim against the company. An accurate balance sheet will reflect these obligations.

### b. Long-Term Liabilities

Claims of outsiders on the business that do not come due within one year are called "long-term liabilities" or, simply, "other liabilities." Included in this category are bonded indebtedness, mortgages, and long-term loans from individuals, banks, and others from whom the business may borrow money, such as the SBA. As was stated before, any part of a long-term debt that falls due within one year from the date of the balance sheet would be recorded as part of the current liabilities of the business.

## Owner's Equity

The owner's equity section of the balance sheet is located on the right-hand side underneath the listing of the liabilities. It shows the claims of the owners on the company. Essentially, this is a balancing figure--that is, the owners get what's left of the assets after the liability claims have been recognized. This is an obvious definition, if you will remember the balance sheet formula. Transposing the formula as we learned it a few minutes ago, it becomes Assets - Liabilities = Owner's Equity. In the case where the business is a sole proprietorship, it is customary to show owner's equity as one entry with no distinction being made between the owner's initial investment and the accumulated retained earnings of the business. However, in the case of an incorporated business, there are entries for stockholders' claims as well as for earnings that have been accumulated and retained in the business. Of course, if the business has been consistently operating at a loss, the proprietor's claim may be less than his initial investment. And, in the case of a corporation, the balancing account could be operating deficit rather than retained earnings.

If we put together the entries we have been talking about, we have a complete balance sheet. There is a lot of information in this statement. It tells you just what you have and where it is. It also tells you what you owe. You need this information to help you decide what actions you should take in running your business. If you need to borrow money, the banker or anyone else from whom you borrow will want to look at your balance sheet.

## D. THE INCOME STATEMENT

In recent years the income statement has become as important as the balance sheet as a financial and management record. It is also called the profit and loss statement, or simply the P and L statement. This financial record summarizes the activities of the company over a period of time, listing those that can be expressed in dollars. That is, it reports the revenues of the company and the expenses incurred in. obtaining the revenues, and it shows the profit or loss resulting from these activities. The income statement complements the balance sheet. While balance sheet analysis shows the change in position of the company at the end of accounting periods, the income statement shows how the change took place during the accounting period. Both reports 'are necessary for a full understanding of the operation of the business.

The income statement for particular company should be tailored to fit the activities of that company, and there is no rigid format that must be followed in constructing this report. But the following categories are found in most income statements.

## 1. Sales

The major activity of most businesses is the sales of products and services, and the bulk of revenue comes from sales. In recording sales, the figure used is net sales-that is, sales after discounts, allowances, and returned goods have been accounted for.

## 2. Cost of Goods Sold

Another important item, in calculating profit or loss, is the cost of the goods that the company has sold. This item is difficult to calculate accurately. Since the goods sold come from inventory, and since the company may have bought parts of its inventory at several prices, it is hard to determine exactly what is the cost of the particular part of the inventory that was sold. In large companies, and particularly in companies using cost accounting, there are some rather complicated methods of determining "cost of goods sold, " but they are beyond the scope of this presentation. However, there is a simple, generally accepted way of calculating cost of goods sold. In this method you simply add the net amount of purchases during the accounting period to your beginning inventory, and subtract from this your ending inventory. The result can be considered cost-of-goods sold.

## 3. Gross Margin

The difference between sales and cost of goods sold is called the "gross margin" or gross profit. This item is often expressed as a percentage of sales, as well as in dollar figures. The percentage gross margin is a very significant figure because it indicates what the average markup is on the merchandise sold. So, if a manager knows his expenses as a percentage of sales, he can calculate the mark up necessary to obtain the gross margin he needs for a profitable operation. It is surprising how many small-business men do not know what basis to use in setting markups. In fact, with the various, allowances, discounts, and markdowns that a business may offer, many managers do not know what their markup actually is. The gross margin calculation on the income statement can help the manager with this problem.

There are other costs of running a business besides the cost of the goods sold. When you use the simple method of determining costs of goods sold, these costs are called "expenses."

For example, here are some typical expenses: salaries and wages, utilities, depreciation, interest, administrative expenses, supplies, bad debts, advertising, and taxes--Federal, State, and local. These are typical expenses, but there are many other kinds of expenses that may be experienced by other businesses. For example, we have shown in the Blank Company's balance sheet that he owns his own land and building--with a mortgage, of course. These accounts for part of his depreciation and interest expenses, but for a company that rents its quarters, rent would appear as the expense item. Other common expenses are traveling expense, commissions, and advertising.

Most of these expense items are self-explanatory, but there are a few that merit further comment. For one thing, the salary or draw of the owner should be recorded among the expenses--either as a part of salaries and wages or as part of administrative expenses. To exclude the owner's compensation from expenses distorts the actual profitability of the business. And, if the company is incorporated, it would reduce the allowable tax deductions of the business. Of course, for tax purposes, the owner's salary or draw in a proprietorship or partnership is considered as part of the net profit.

We discussed depreciation when we examined the balance sheet, and we mentioned that it was an item of expense. Although no money is actually paid out for depreciation, it is a real expense because it represents reduction in the value of the assets.

The most important thing about expenses is to be sure to include all of the expenses that the business incurs. This not only helps the owner get a more accurate picture of his operation but it allows him to take full advantage of the tax deductions that legitimate expenses offer.

## 4. Net Profit

In a typical company when expenses are subtracted from gross margin, the remainder is profit. However, if the business receives revenue from sources other than sales, such as rents, dividends on securities held by the company, or interest on money loaned by the company, it is added to profit at this point. For bookkeeping purposes, the resulting profit is labeled "profit before taxes." This is the figure from which Federal income taxes are figured. If the business is a proprietorship, the profit is taxed as part of the owner's income. If the business is a corporation, the profits may be taxed on the basis of the corporate income tax schedule. When income taxes have been accounted for, the resultant entry is called "net profit after taxes," or simply "net profit." This is usually the final entry on the income statement.

Another financial record which managers can use to advantage is the funds flow statement. This statement is also called statement of sources and uses of funds and sometimes the "where got--where gone" statement. Whatever you call it, a record of sources and uses of past funds is useful to the manager. He can use it to evaluate past performance, and as a guide in determining future uses and sources of money.

When we speak of "funds" we do not necessarily mean actual "dollars" or "cash." Although accounting records are all written in monetary terms, they do not always involve an exchange of money. Many times in business transactions, it is credit rather than dollars that changes hands. Therefore, when we speak of funds flow, we are speaking of exchanges of *economic values* rather than merely the physical flow of dollars.

Basically, funds are used to: increase assets and reduce liabilities. They are also sometimes used to reduce owner's equity. An example of this would be the use of company funds to buy up outstanding stock or to buy out a partner. Where do funds come from? The three basic sources of funds are a reduction in assets, increases in liabilities, and increased owner's equity. All balance sheet items can be affected by the obtaining and spending of company fund's.

To examine the construction and use of a funds flow statement, let's take another look at the Blank Company. Here we show comparative balance sheets for two one-year periods. For the sake of simplicity, we have included only selected items from the balance sheets for analysis. Notice that the company gained funds by:

reducing cash $300,

increasing accounts payable $400,

putting $500 more owner's equity in the business, and

plowing back $800 of the profit into the business.

These funds were used to:

increase accounts receivable $300,
increase inventory $200,

buy $500 worth of equipment, and

pay off $1, 000 worth of long-term debt.

This funds flow statement has indicated to Mr. Blank where he has gotten his funds and how he has spent them. He can analyze these figures in the light of his plans and objectives and take appropriate action.

For example, if Mr. Blank wants to answer the question "Should I buy new capital equipment?" a look at his funds flow statement would show him his previous sources of funds, and it would give him a clue as to whether he could obtain funds for any new equipment.

## I V. OTHER RECORDS

Up to this point, we have been talking about the basic types of bookkeeping records. In addition, we have discussed the two basic financial statements of a business: the balance sheet and the profit and loss statement. Now let us give our attention briefly to some other records which are very helpful to running a business successfully.

One element that appears on the balance sheet which I believe we can agree is important is cash. Because it is the lifeblood of all business, cash should be controlled and safe-guarded at all times. The daily summary of sales and cash receipts and the checkbook are used by many manager s of small businesses to help provide that control.

### A. Daily Summary of Sales and Cash. Receipts

Not all businesses summarize their daily transactions. However, a daily summary of sales and cash receipts is a very useful tool for checking how your business is doing on a day-to-day basis. At the close of each day's business, the actual cash on hand is counted and "balanced" against the total of the receipts recorded for the day. This balancing is done by means of the Daily Summary of Sales and Cash Receipts. This is a recording of every cash 'receipt and every charge sale, whether you use a cash register or sales checks or both. If you have more than one cash register, a daily summary should be prepared for each; the individual cash-register summaries can then be combined into one overall summary for convenience in handling.

In the daily summary form used for purposes of illustration, (see Handout), the first section, "Cash Receipts," records the total of all cash taken in during the day from whatever source. This is the cash that must be accounted for over and above, the amount in the change and/ or petty cash funds. We shall touch upon these two funds later. The three components of cash receipts are (1) cash sales, (2) collections on accounts, and (3) miscellaneous receipts.

The daily total of cash sales is obtained from a cash-register tape reading or, if no cash register is used, by totaling the cash-sales checks.

For collections on accounts, an individual record of each customer payment on account should be kept, whether or not these collections are rung up on a cash register. The amount to be entered on the daily summary is obtained by totaling these individual records.

Miscellaneous receipts are daily cash transactions that cannot be classified as sales or collections. They might include refunds from suppliers for overpayment, advertising rebates or allowances, . collections of rent from sub-leases or concessions, etc. Like collections on account, a sales check or memo should be made out each time such cash is taken in.

The total of daily cash receipts to be accounted for on the daily summary is obtained by adding cash sales, collections on account, and miscellaneous receipts.

The second section, "Cash on Hand," of a daily summary is a count of the cash actually on hand plus the cash that is represented by petty cash slips. The daily summary provides for counts of your total coins, bills, and checks as well as the amount expended for petty cash. The latter is determined by adding the amounts on the individual petty cash slips. By totaling all four of these counts, you obtain the total cash accounted for. To determine the amount of your daily cash deposit, you deduct from the "total cash accounted for" the total of the petty cash and change funds.

Cash to be deposited on the daily summary should always equal the total receipts to be accounted for minus the fixed amount of your petty cash and change funds. If it does not, all the work in preparing the daily summary should be carefully checked. Obviously, an error in giving change, in ringing up a sale, or neglecting to do so, will result in a cash shortage or overage. The daily summary provides spaces for such errors so that the proper entries can be made in your bookkeeping records. The last section of your daily summary, "Sales," records the total daily sales broken down into (1) cash sales and (2) charge sales.

As soon as possible after the daily summary has been completed, all cash for deposit should be taken to the bank. A duplicate deposit slip, stamped by the bank, should be kept with the daily summary as evidence that the deposit was made.

## B. Petty Cash and Charge Funds

The record of, daily, sales and cash. Receipts which we have just described. is designed. on the assumption that a petty cash fund and a change cash fund, or a combination change and petty cash fund, are used. All businesses, small and large, have day-to-day expenses that are so small they do not warrant the drawing of a check. Good management practice calls for careful control of such expenses. The petty cash fund provides such control. It is a sum of money which is obtained by drawing a check to provide several days, a week's, or a month's need of cash for small purchases. The type of business will determine the amount of the petty cash fund.

Each time a payment is made from the petty cash, a slip should be made out. If an invoice or receipt is available, it should be attached to the petty- cash slip. The slips and the money ordinarily, but not necessarily, are kept separate from other currency in your cash till, drawer, or register. At all times, the total of unspent petty cash and petty cash slips should equal the fixed amount of the fund. When the total of the slips approaches the fixed amount of the petty cash fund, a check is drawn for the total amount of the slips. The money from this check is used to bring the fund back to its fixed amount.

In addition to a petty cash fund, some businesses that receive cash in over-the-counter transactions have a change fund. The amount needed for making change varies with the size and type of business, and, in some cases, with the days of the week. Control of the money in your change fund will be made-easier, however, if you set a fixed amount large enough to meet all the ordinary change-making needs of your business. Each day, when the day's receipts are balanced and prepared for a bank deposit, you will retain bills and coins totaling the fixed amount of the fund for use the following day. Since you had that amount on hand before you made the day's first sale, the entire amount of the day's receipts will still be available for your bank deposit.

In some cases, the petty cash fund is kept in a petty cash box or safe, apart from the change fund. However, the same fund can serve for both petty cash and change. For example, if you decide that you need $50 for making change and $25 for petty cash, one $75 fund can be used. Whenever, in balancing the day's operations, you see that the petty cash slips total more than $25, you can write a petty cash check for the amount of the slips.

## C. Record of Cash Disbursement

To safeguard your cash, it is recommended that all receipts be deposited in a bank account and that all disbursements, except those made from the petty cash fund, are made by drawing a check on that account. Your bank account should be used exclusively for business transactions. If your business is typical, you will have to write checks for merchandise purchases, employee's salaries, rent, utilities, payroll taxes, petty cash, and various other expenses. Your check stubs will serve as a record of cash disbursements.

The checkbook stub should contain all the details of the disbursement including the date, payee, amount and purpose of the payment. In addition, a running balance of the amount you have in your bank account should be maintained by subtracting the amount of each check from the existing balance after the previous check was drawn. If the checks of your checkbook are prenumbered, it is important to mark plainly in the stub when a check is voided for one reason or another.

Each check should have some sort of written document to support it--an invoice, petty-cash voucher, payroll summary and so on. Supporting documents should be approved by you or someone you have authorized before a check is drawn. They should be marked paid and filed after the check is drawn.

Periodically, your bank will send you a statement of your account and return cancelled checks for which money has been withdrawn from your account. It is important that you reconcile your records with those of the bank. This means that the balances in your checkbook and on the bank statement should agree. Uncashed checks must be deducted from your checkbook balance and deposits not recorded on the bank statement must be added to its balance in order to get both balances to agree.

## D . Accounts Receivable Records

If you extend credit to your customers, you must keep an accurate account of your credit sales not only in total as you have done on the daily summary but also by the amount that each individual customer owes you. Moreover, you must be systematic about billings and collections. This is important. It results in better relations with your charge customers and in fewer losses from bad debts.

The simplest method of handling accounts receivable--other than just keeping a file of sales-slip carbons--is to have an account sheet for each credit customer. Charge sales and payments on charge sales are posted to each customer sheet. Monthly billing to each of your charge customers should be made from their individual account sheets.

At least two or three times a year, your accounts receivable should be aged. You do this by posting each customer's account and his unpaid charges in columns according to age. These columns are labeled: not due; 1 to 30 days past due; 31 to 60 days past due; 61 to 90 days past due; etc. This analysis will indicate those customers who are not complying with your credit terms.

## E . Property Records and Depreciation

In every type of business, it is necessary to purchase property and equipment from time to time. This property usually will last for several years, so it would be unrealistic to show the total amount of the purchase as an expense in any one year. Therefore, when this property is set up in the books as an asset, records must be kept to decrease its value over its life. This decrease is known as depreciation. I have mentioned this before during this talk. The amount of the decrease in value in one year, that is, the depreciation, is charged as an expense for the year.

I am talking about this expense, particularly, because no cash is paid out for it. It is a non-cash, not-out-of-pocket expense. You don't have to hand over actual money at the end of the month.

Records should be kept of this because, otherwise, there is a danger that this expense will be overlooked. Yet it is impossible to figure true profit or loss without considering it. When you deduct the depreciation expense from your firm's income, you reduce your tax liabilities. When you put this depreciation expense into a depreciation allowance account, you are keeping score on your "debt" to depreciation.

In a barber shop, to take a simple example, depreciation of its chairs, dryers, and clippers at the end of the year amounts to $136. You deduct this $136 from the shop's income, in this case, to pay the debt credited to your depreciation allowance account. Since this equipment has the same depreciation value each year, the depreciation allowance account at the end of 3 years will show that a total of $408 worth of equipment has been used up. The books of the barbershop therefore show an expense of $408 which actually has not been spent. It is in the business to replace the depreciated equipment. If replacement will not take place in the immediate future, the money can be used in inventory, or in some other way to generate more sales or profits.

How you handle this money depends on many things. You can set it aside at a low interest rate and have that much less operating money. Or you can put it to work in your business where it will help to keep your finances healthy.

Remember, however, that you must be prepared financially when it is time to buy replacement equipment. A depreciation allowance account on your books can help to keep you aware of this. It helps you keep score on how much depreciation or replacement money you are using in your business.

Keeping score with a depreciation allowance account helps you to know when you need to convert some of your assets into replacement cash. If, for example, you know on January 1 that Your delivery truck will be totally depreciated by June 30, you can review the situation objectively. You can decide whether you ought to use the truck longer or replace it. If you decide to replace it, then you can plan to accumulate the cash, and time the purchase in order to make the best deal.

### F. Schedule of Insurance Coverage

The schedule of insurance coverage is prepared to indicate the type of coverage and the amount presently in force. This schedule should list all the insurance carried by your business-- fire and extended coverage, theft, liability, life, business interruption and so forth.

This schedule should be prepared to present the following: name of insurance company, annual premium, expiration date, type of coverage, amount of coverage, asset insured, and estimated current value of asset insured.

An analysis of this schedule should indicate the adequacy of insurance coverage. A review of this schedule with your insurance agent is suggested.

## V. CONCLUSION

During the brief time allotted to this subject of the basic fundamentals of bookkeeping, we have just scratched its surface. What we have tried to do is to inform you, as small-business managers, of the importance of good records. We have described the components of the important records that you must have if you are going to manage your business efficiently and profitably. In addition, we have brought to your attention some of the subsidiary records that will aid you in managing your business.

There are other records such as breakeven charts, budgets, cost accounting systems, to mention a few, which can also benefit the progressive manager. However, we do not have the time even to give you the highlights of those management tools. Your accountant can assist you in learning to understand and use them. Moreover, he can help you to develop and use the records we have discussed. For further information about them, you also can read the publications of the Small Business Administration, some of which are available to you free of charge.

By reading and using the accounting advice available to you, you can make sure that you have the right records to improve your managing skill and thereby increase your profits.

---